WHAT PEOPLE ARE SA[illegible]

MOON SUR[illegible]

"In today's challenging times, teenagers need all the help and su[illegible]port they can get and Nikki has provided the perfect h[illegible]book in Moonsurfing for Teens. Practical advice in a magical [illegible] I highly recommend it."
Jacky [illegible]ewcomb, Sunday Times Best Selling author of *An Angel Saved My Life*

Moon Surfing is a brilliantly written and essential guide to astrology for teens, young people and beginners of all ages too. *Moon Surfing* introduces a complex subject, making it fun, entertaining and accessible to all. A must have book for any budding young astrologers or the astro curious out there!
Alice Grist, Author of *The High Heeled Guide to Spiritual Living* (Best Book - Prediction Magazine Awards 2011)

"A superbly common-sense astrology book with lots of relevant information to help troubled teens cope with everything from breaking-up with boyfriends to making new friends.

Nikki has done a wonderful job of constructing and interpreting a birth chart using easy-to-follow information and useful website references. This is quite advanced astrological information broken down into easily digestible bite-sized steps so even the most shy astrological student can successfully follow the path of the Moon in their life."
Mary English, Astrological Author of *How to Survive a Pisces*

Thoughtful, insightful and with her finger firmly on the cosmic pulse, Nikki is the definitive astrological guide to see you through your tricky teen years.

Anna McCleery, Producer BBC Slink/Founder of Whatever After.co.uk

Moon Surfing

A Lunar Astrology Handbook for Teens

Moon Surfing

A Lunar Astrology Handbook for Teens

Nikki Harper

Winchester, UK
Washington, USA

First published by Dodona Books, 2012
Dodona Books is an imprint of John Hunt Publishing Ltd., Laurel House, Station Approach,
Alresford, Hants, SO24 9JH, UK
office1@jhpbooks.net
www.johnhuntpublishing.com
www.dodona-books.com

For distributor details and how to order please visit the 'Ordering' section on our website.

ISBN: 978 1 78099 326 3

A CIP catalogue record for this book is available from the British Library.

Design: Stuart Davies

Printed and bound by CPI Group (UK) Ltd, Croydon, CR0 4YY

CONTENTS

Introduction

Your Moon Journal

Why Keep a Moon Journal?

You're a busy girl with many demands on your time. Keeping a moon journal sounds like just one more chore, right? Wrong. Moon astrology is a living, vibrant system you can use to chart your emotions, moods and daily challenges as – and before – they happen. In astrology, the Moon rules instincts, emotions and intuition. Its swift passage through the zodiac each month forms a natural pattern of events, a cycle of highs and lows which you can easily learn to anticipate and to mould to your own advantage. Learning about your Moon Sign and house will help you to understand yourself better, but that's only the beginning – using a Moon journal will help you to understand exactly how the changing Moon cycle works for you, at home, at school, in your love life and your health. Before long, you'll start to notice patterns emerging – perhaps you always row with your parents when the Moon is in your 9th House, while homework is a breeze during the New Moon. Being forewarned is forearmed, even if you have to make a habit of a long, soothing bath during that tricky 9th House Moon and pin a reminder to your mirror to count to ten before opening your mouth!

What You Need

To get started with your Moon journal, you don't need very much at all. Your journal can take any form you like, from an exercise book to a loose-leaf folder or ring binder. I recommend using loose pages in a ring binder because that makes it easy to add pages at a later date, to rearrange and reorganise the sections if you're trying to spot patterns and to journal as and when you feel like it without being intimidated by a whole book full of blank space. Page dividers are handy for separating out the different sections of your journal. You'll find a wealth of free, downloadable pages for a ring binder moon journal at the website accompanying this book.

You'll also need Internet access. At http://spiritodyssey.com /moonsurfing/ you can download ready made journal pages to use if you don't want to create your own, and you can also visit Moon Surfing's Facebook page at http://www.facebook.com/ Moon Surfing to get help or advice or to share your thoughts with others. You'll also need to be online to use my recommended websites to find your astrological data; you could do this manually with an ephemeris, but it's a lot more difficult.

The Parts of Your Moon Journal

Once up and running, your moon journal will consist of several different parts. Right at the front will be your Lunar Personality pages with information about your natal Moon Sign and house – this is the key to your emotional personality and the basis for all of the rest of your observations. Next, you will have a Moon Cycles section with journal pages and worksheets for the Full Moon, New Moon and eclipses. Then come sections for the different areas of your life such as school, home, love and health – you'll be adding notes here as the Moon affects each of these areas in turn. Finally comes the Daily Moon Journal section, with a page for each day you remember to use your journal, charting your moods, emotions and daily events.

Getting Started with Your Moon Journal

The very first thing you need to do is to calculate the position of your natal moon – exactly where in the sky the Moon was at the time and place of your birth. Fortunately, this is now easy to do with many online sites offering a fast, accurate answer. Having found out the sign of your natal moon, you'll also need to either find out or calculate its house position – how to do this and what it all means is fully explained in the next chapter.

Getting Creative

If you're the arty type, you can have a lot of fun designing a cover page for your binder. I'd suggest waiting until you've completed the Lunar Personality pages and found out about your Moon Sign. Inspired by this, you might like to draw or paint or craft a cover which explores what your Moon Sign means to you. Over time, you can also use your moon journal as a kind of scrapbook – feel free to paste in photographs, clippings, mementos and artwork that you feel is relevant to the page in question. Your moon journal is entirely personal to you – some people like a relatively plain, business-like approach with minimal decoration, others like to really go to town and turn it into a mini artwork in its own right. Whatever feels right to you is perfect.

Keeping Your Moon Journal Regularly

If you've never kept a journal before, it's not always easy to get into the habit. Very often, people start in a flurry of enthusiasm, promising themselves that they'll write every day… and then end up in a state of disillusion when they find themselves with huge gaps in the journal. This is another reason why a loose-leaf binder is a good idea – it makes the gaps much less obvious! In truth, you don't necessarily need to use your journal every day to reap the benefits. The more you use it the more you'll learn about yourself and the more in tune with the Moon's dance you'll become, but even using it once a week or so is better than nothing at all. If you do find that you lapse but want to get back into using it, aim for a New Moon to restart your journaling habit – and don't beat yourself up about it!

So, now you know the basics about why keeping a moon journal is a good idea and about the kinds of pages and information we're going to put in it. Let's get started with the nitty gritty and find out about YOUR Lunar Personality!

Chapter 1

Your Lunar Personality

There are two simple steps to finding out about your lunar personality. First of all, you need to find out what sign the Moon was in at the date, time and place of your birth. That will be your Moon Sign and we'll work on that in this chapter. In the next chapter, you will find out which house of the astrological chart the Moon occupied – your Moon House. These two pieces of information together form the basis of your whole Moon Journal and hold the key to your emotional personality. Let's get started!

What is a Moon Sign?

You're probably familiar with the term Sun Sign, meaning the zodiac sign occupied by the Sun at the moment and place of your birth. You will no doubt identify with some of the commonly known traits of your Sun Sign – but usually not all of them. That's because astrology is much more than just a Sun Sign and your complex personality is a blend of all of the planets and many of the signs.

When you were born, the Moon was occupying a zodiac sign, just as the Sun and all of the other planets were. In contrast to the Sun, which typically spends approximately a month in each sign, the Moon passes through an entire zodiac sign in just two and a half days, making a complete tour of the zodiac in just under a month. People born during the same month as you will have either your Sun Sign or the one before it, but could have any one of the twelve Moon Signs. If you've always wondered why your friend has the same Sun Sign as you but is very different, it's very likely that you have contrasting Moon Signs.

In astrology, your Moon Sign relates to your innermost

nature, your instincts, moods and emotional needs. It's often considered to be the real you – the one that shows through either at times of stress or in moments of relaxation, as opposed to the Sun Sign mask you wear when you present yourself to others.

The needs and desires of your Moon Sign or your lunar personality must be taken care of and satisfied before you can make progress in life. If something is working against your lunar personality, you will feel it as a deep-seated unease or a niggling worry. Being able to adjust your circumstances to feed and honour your lunar personality leads to a greater feeling of contentment and happiness and the kind of feel-good factor so many of us spend our lives searching for.

Finding Out Your Moon Sign

Calculating an astrology chart by hand is a long and complicated affair, beyond the scope of this book. Fortunately, in this cyber age, there are plenty of websites which will provide you with free, personalised astrological information. There are just two key pieces of information we need to establish: your Moon position and your Ascendant position (we'll talk about the Ascendant later). In the event that you don't know your Sun Sign, this process will also give you that information. Here's how:

1. You know what date you were born, right? See, that one's simple!
2. If you're not already certain, find out the town or city you were born in. If you were born in the middle of nowhere, what was the nearest town?
3. This is the trickier bit – what time, exactly, were you born? Often parents will remember this or perhaps it's noted on your first photograph or a commemorative plaque. If you were born in Scotland, you're fortunate because it will be recorded on your birth certificate. Don't panic if you can't find out an exact time. The more specific the better, but

even something like "mid morning" or "around tea time" will help.

4 Visit one of these websites. I recommend Café Astrology if you were born in the UK and Astrodienst if you were born elsewhere. The About.com link can be used if either of the other two sites are unavailable. Café Astrology – http://astro.cafeastrology.com/cgi-bin/astro/natal
Astrodienst – http://www.astro.com ~ in the left hand menu click on "Free Horoscopes" and then choose "Horoscope Drawings and Calculations", then "Chart Drawing, Ascendant".
About.com – http://www.astrology.about.com – click on "Free Birth Chart".

5 On your chosen site, input your date of birth, followed by your place and time of birth. If you don't have the exact time, approximate as best as you can. Enter 10.30 am, for instance, if your parents say mid morning, or ask them what time they used to eat if they say you arrived just in time for tea! If you are using Astrodienst, DO NOT check the time unknown box.

6 The site will then present your chart details on screen. Keep it on screen or print it out, as you will need some of this information now and some in the next chapter.

Don't worry if all that looks complicated. It's a simple process once you get started and shouldn't take you longer than ten minutes. If for any reason you can't follow the steps above, you can contact me (Moon Surfing's Facebook page is probably your best bet) and I will calculate both your Moon position and your Ascendant position for you. I recommend trying the steps above first, however, as it may take me a little while to get back to you but online you can receive the answer straight away.

Different sites present the data in different ways, but what you are looking for, among your data, is something like this –

although of course, your figures will be different to my examples:

Café Astrology ~ Moon Cancer 11.54, Ascendant Scorpio 17.34

Astrodienst ~ Moon 11 Canc 54. To see the Ascendant here, look on the chart wheel at the 9 o'clock position; you will see a zodiac sign symbol and it will be marked as AC 17 34.

About.com ~ Scroll down to the text underneath chart wheel. There you will see Moon 11 degrees Cancer, Rising Sign (this is another name for Ascendant) 17 degrees Scorpio.

Whatever site you've used, the zodiac sign mentioned with the Moon is your Moon Sign. There you go! You're now ready to record this vital piece of information in your Moon Journal. You can make a page about it yourself, if you like, or you can download my Lunar Personality sheet from http://spiritodyssey.com/moonsurfing/ and begin to fill it in there. Let's take a wander through the Moon Signs before we move on to discovering your Moon House.

Your Moon Sign: The Key to Your Emotional Personality

Moon in Aries

An instinctive need for action means that you feel happiest on the go. Hanging around, waiting for others to do things will infuriate you and you strongly believe that you can – and should – take the lead. Aries energy is fast, impulsive and sometimes reckless. Through the filter of the Moon, this translates into hot-headed emotional responses and often quite a bit of drama over emotional concerns. Your temper is quick to rise, but equally quick to dissipate – sometimes not before the damage is done, however. Sometimes a little accident-prone, you tend to act before you think things through.

The word no is not in the Aries Moon vocabulary. Not only will you refuse to be told what to do, but you'll also refuse to accept that what you want is not possible. With incredible levels of determination and sheer force of will, you have the knack of making things happen. You're an initiator and an inspiration to those around you.

You're very decisive and can't see the point in endless agonising over decisions. A lack of patience with others who *do* see the point sometimes means a rocky relationship with family and friends, but you would instinctively move heaven and earth to protect those you love – they can *always* count on you when it matters most.

Your Emotional Needs: Independence, freedom, speed

Your Emotional Strengths: Courage, passion, determination

Your Emotional Challenges: Selfishness, recklessness, impatience

Working with your Aries Moon: How much of this description resonates with you? Be honest! If your Sun Sign is very different to Aries, remember that these Moon Sign traits are often not on display except to those who know you best or when you're under pressure. Try these writing prompts on your Lunar Personality page:

- You need independence, freedom and speed of action. In what areas of your life do you feel those needs are satisfied? Is there a part of your life where your independence is being stifled? Why?
- Write about a time when you showed courage, passion or determination. How did that make you feel? Were others around you surprised by your actions?
- Think about something you have done which was selfish, reckless or overly impatient. How did it turn out? How did you feel afterwards?

Moon in Taurus

Security is your major emotional motivation. You thrive against a background where you know what's what and what to expect from each facet of your life. Because you value the status quo so highly, you react defensively when you feel change is on the horizon; this resistance to change is so deep-rooted that you'll resist even what you know to be beneficial improvements to "the way things are done around here".

Taurus energy is stubborn and tenacious, and once you're in a frame of mind, it takes a great deal of effort to get out of it. Although possessive and perhaps a little selfish, you do boast a very open, tolerant mind and a great deal of compassion and kindness. Your common sense is a huge asset and you're not the type to be overly stressed by imaginary worries.

The "good life" theme is evident in your lifestyle too, as you love to surround yourself with fine things, beautiful clothes and good food. Prone to comfort eating, your health can suffer if your emotional needs are not met. When all is well, your warmth and humour shine through and you can be the most loving, sensible and dependable of friends.

Your Emotional Needs: Stability, constancy, comfortable lifestyle

Your Emotional Strengths: Reliability, common sense, tenacity

Your Emotional Challenges: Stubbornness, overly materialistic attitude, rigidity

Working with your Taurus Moon: How much of this description resonates with you? Be honest! If your Sun Sign is very different to Taurus, remember that these Moon Sign traits are often not on display except to those who know you best or when you're under pressure. Try these writing prompts on your Lunar Personality page:

- You need stability, emotional security and a sense of richness. In what areas of your life do you feel those needs are satisfied? Is there a part of your life where your security is being compromised? Why?
- Write about a time when you showed common sense, tolerance or determination. How did that make you feel? Were others around you surprised by your actions?
- Think about something you have done which was overly

materialistic or a time when you refused to budge from your stance no matter what. How did it turn out? How did you feel afterwards?

Moon in Gemini

Fast, lively emotional reactions are the key to understanding the Gemini Moon. You're very talkative and you talk very quickly too, especially when under stress. With a mind which constantly jumps from one thought to the next, it's easy for you to do a dozen things at once – in fact, you struggle to focus on just one. Although almost everything interests you, you bore quickly and are always on the look out for the next big thing.

Gemini energy is very rational and logical so you often analyse your feelings or even censor them. Not given to bursts of emotion, you tend to keep your stronger feelings bottled up inside, not sure what to do with them or even being ashamed of them. It's hard for you to reconcile the way you feel with the way you think you ought to feel, which can lead to inner conflict.

Your emotions are quite fickle and you're prone to switching allegiances rather suddenly, which others find hard to fathom. Energetic, quick to communicate and equally quick to change your mind, you're a fascinating friend but sometimes hard work for friends and family to understand due to your cool and distant demeanour.

Your Emotional Needs: Variety, an outlet for analysing emotions

Your Emotional Strengths: Logic, communication, flexibility

Your Emotional Challenges: Fickleness, unwillingness to follow instincts

Working with your Gemini Moon: How much of this description resonates with you? Be honest! If your Sun Sign is very different to Gemini, remember that these Moon Sign traits are often not on display except to those who know you best or when you're under pressure. Try these writing prompts on your Lunar Personality page:

- You need variety and some way of rationalising your emotions. In what areas of your life do you feel those needs are satisfied? Do you keep a diary or talk regularly to someone close about how you feel? Is there a part of your life where variety is hard to find? Why?
- Write about a time when you showed great flexibility or where your logic or communication skills worked to your advantage. How did that make you feel? Were others around you surprised by your actions?
- Think about something you have done which was overly fickle or a time when you refused to listen to your instincts when you perhaps should have done. How did it turn out? How did you feel afterwards?

Moon in Cancer

Your emotional instinct, first and foremost, is to protect yourself and those dear to you. This defensiveness is evident in your whole approach to life and you are a cautious, careful person as a rule. Very emotional and intuitive, you do listen to your instincts and you are normally well served by following your gut feelings, which rarely let you down.

A very strong imagination is both a blessing and a curse, because although it lends a wonderfully creative edge to your nature, your tendency to worry means that minor niggles can be blown up out of all proportion as your default setting is to imagine the worst rather than the best. Your emotional security is firmly rooted in the family and Cancer energy is also strongly attached to the past. A bit of a collector, you tend to hoard nostalgic items from your childhood or from previous generations, striving for a tangible connection with what has gone before.

Loved ones may find your mood swings difficult to deal with and when you feel down it's very hard for you to shake off negativity. Nonetheless, your sensitivity and kindness are legendary and you love to feel needed, which makes you an excellent homemaker, caregiver, friend and companion.

Your Emotional Needs: Close family ties, someone to "mother", roots

Your Emotional Strengths: Imagination, sensitivity, protectiveness

Your Emotional Challenges: Moodiness, anxiety, being stuck in the past

Working with your Cancer Moon: How much of this description resonates with you? Be honest! If your Sun Sign is very different to Cancer, remember that these Moon Sign traits are often not on display except to those who know you best or when you're under pressure. Try these writing prompts on your Lunar Personality page:

- You need close family ties and a sense of belonging. In what areas of your life do you feel those needs are satisfied? Is there a part of your life where you feel cut off or a bit of an outsider? Why?
- Write about a time when you showed imagination or sensitivity or a time when you protected someone emotionally, verbally or even physically. How did that make you feel? Were others around you surprised by your actions?
- Think about a time when your moodiness was a problem or about a situation which made you feel very anxious. How did it turn out? How did you feel afterwards?

Moon in Leo

You're confident, expressive and ambitious, although whether your confidence is genuine or more a smokescreen to hide insecurities depends upon the rest of your astrological chart. With exceptional charisma and leadership talents, you make a very immediate impression upon those around you, but your extrovert nature can sometimes come across as showing off or arrogance. You have an opinion on everything and are never slow to come forward with it, but being dogmatic about your stance can lead others to regard you as stubborn and close-minded.

Your healthy imagination is expressed with creative Leo energy, and an inner determination ensures that you keep trying until you get where you want to be. Intuition is strong too, but in the rush to be seen you do sometimes overlook that nagging inner voice.

Leo energy is also dramatic, flamboyant and generous, but you have a sense of entitlement which can lead to many a scene if you feel that you are being overlooked or that your rightful place has been taken by someone else. Nonetheless, your cheerful demeanour soon erases those tantrums and in general you are perceived as fun and larger than life.

Your Emotional Needs: Attention, to be in charge, to be adored

Your Emotional Strengths: Creativity, generosity, exuberance

Your Emotional Challenges: Arrogance, drama queen, dogmatic

Working with your Leo Moon: How much of this description resonates with you? Be honest! If your Sun Sign is very different to Leo, remember that these Moon Sign traits are often not on display except to those who know you best or when you're under pressure. Try these writing prompts on your Lunar Personality page:

- You need to be made to feel special and to feel in charge of your life. In what areas of your life do you feel those needs are satisfied? Is there a part of your life where you feel powerless or overlooked? Why?
- Write about a time when your creativity or exuberance won the day, or when you showed imagination or sensitivity or a time when you were particularly generous towards someone. How did that make you feel? Were others around you surprised by your actions?
- Think about a time when your refusal to hear another point

of view was a problem, or about a time when you created a drama unnecessarily. How did it turn out? How did you feel afterwards?

Moon in Virgo

Tending towards a somewhat nervous or shy disposition, you are prone to deep-seated worries and anxieties, even when you know they are not rational. You do, however, have a great deal of common sense and a very practical, sensible outlook on life. Listening to your deepest emotions is uncomfortable for you, which can lead to stress related health issues.

Communication is an exceptional talent of yours, especially in writing and you love literature and books. With an incisive mind and a dry wit, you are a formidable opponent in a debate and can stand firmly on your own two feet in any argument, even though you may be quaking inside.

Virgo energy is quite critical and with the Moon in Virgo the danger is that the criticism is all turned inwards, towards yourself. You can frequently be your own worst enemy and you hold yourself to much higher standards than you hold those around you. Analysing your every mood and feeling can become a habit. Because you like to be in control of your emotions, it's difficult for people to see through to the real you as you protect yourself well. Nonetheless, hard-working, modest and genuine, you are a valued friend, loved for your sincerity.

Your Emotional Needs: Privacy, to keep your emotions to yourself

Your Emotional Strengths: Analytical ability, cool head

Your Emotional Challenges: Worry, lack of confidence, self-criticism

Working with your Virgo Moon: How much of this description resonates with you? Be honest! If your Sun Sign is very different to Virgo, remember that these Moon Sign traits are often not on display except to those who know you best or when you're under pressure. Try these writing prompts on your Lunar Personality page:

- You need time and space to deal with your emotions in your own way rather than in public. In what areas of your life do you feel this need is satisfied? Is there a part of your life where you feel uncomfortably exposed or under pressure to reveal too much? Why?
- Write about a time when you kept calm in a crisis and resolved the problem through your common sense, or about a time when you carefully analysed all options before coming to a decision. How did that make you feel? Were others around you surprised by your actions?
- Think about a time when your shyness was a problem or about a time when your self-criticism held you back from doing something you really would have liked to do. How did it turn out? How did you feel afterwards?

Moon in Libra

For you, it's all about balance and harmony. You cannot bear discord and will go out of your way to smooth over differences of opinion in those around you, even to the lengths of lying about your own feelings and views. Calm and generally quite serene in manner, people look to you as a peacemaker and diplomat and, on the surface at least, it takes a great deal to make you lose your cool.

Empathy is strong in this Moon Sign and you easily identify with others' problems. Sometimes, however, you find it difficult to detach yourself from a tricky situation and end up far more involved in it than you wanted to be. Sympathetic, kind and a good listener, you put people at their ease and find it easy to charm others in a social setting.

Because your natural instinct is to make peace, you do struggle with decision-making and are often pulled in opposing directions by friends and family. In trying too hard to be all things to all people, the real you is occasionally lost beneath your wardrobe of masks. What the Libra Moon really wants is frequently not what she ends up bringing about.

Your Emotional Needs: Balance, harmony, calm

Your Emotional Strengths: Diplomacy, kindness, charm

Your Emotional Challenges: Insincerity, loss of identity, indecision

Working with your Libra Moon: How much of this description resonates with you? Be honest! If your Sun Sign is very different to Libra, remember that these Moon Sign traits are often not on display except to those who know you best or when you're under pressure. Try these writing prompts on your Lunar Personality page:

- You need harmony and calm in all areas of your life. In what areas of your life do you feel those needs are satisfied? Is there a part of your life where you feel there is constant discord or where you cannot help to restore serenity? Why?
- Write about a time when someone remarked upon your kindness or when you successfully brought about a resolution to a conflict. How did that make you feel? Were others around you surprised by your actions?
- Think about a time when you went along with a decision you disagreed with for the sake of peace, or when you found yourself saying things you didn't really mean in order to please someone else. How did it turn out? How did you feel afterwards?

Moon in Scorpio

Extremely potent and powerful emotions bubbling just beneath the surface make it very easy for you to overreact to any situation. You are prone to both extreme highs and extreme lows of feeling, but these vivid emotions spur you on to achieve a great deal and are the source of your driven and ambitious nature. You can be somewhat unforgiving of those around you and at times even cruel, although normally in a cruel to be kind context.

Jealousy is one of your most basic, instinctive responses. Very aware of yourself, you know you are being unreasonable at times, but you simply cannot stop yourself. When your strong emotions are channelled towards good, however, such as when you are working towards an ambition, you have a tremendous amount of power, resourcefulness and inner strength. You value privacy very highly and can be quite secretive, even over the most mundane of matters.

You have a penetrating insight into the minds and actions of others and can use this to your advantage in quite a manipulative way. Sometimes spiteful or resentful and never one to forget and forgive, you are nonetheless immensely loyal and very courageous when it matters most.

Your Emotional Needs: Goals, an intense hobby or focus for emotions

Your Emotional Strengths: Insight, determination, passion

Your Emotional Challenges: Jealousy, resentfulness, spite

Working with your Scorpio Moon: How much of this description resonates with you? Be honest! If your Sun Sign is very different to Scorpio, remember that these Moon Sign traits are often not on display except to those who know you best or when you're under pressure. Try these writing prompts on your Lunar Personality page:

- You need ambitions and goals to work towards in order to have a positive outlet for such strong energies. Do you have plenty to work towards and are you able to do so? Is there a part of your life where you feel that you are drifting or where you cannot express your emotions? Why?
- Write about a time when you showed great determination

or insight into how someone else was feeling. How did that make you feel? Were others around you surprised by your actions?

- Think about a time when your jealousy or resentfulness was a problem or about a time when you acted spitefully. How did it turn out? How did you feel afterwards?

Moon in Sagittarius

Overwhelming enthusiasm and optimism are the signatures of this Moon placing. Enjoyment of life is your primary goal and all of your instinctive reactions are focused on providing you with fun, freedom and a challenge to get your teeth into. You embrace change and find yourself easily bored. You'll kick against any restrictions on your behaviour and you are always absolutely determined to be yourself.

Sagittarian energy is impatient and you don't have much time for the social niceties of life, which can lead others to find you a little gruff and overbearing. Intelligent and quick-witted, you love to learn and will seize educational opportunities throughout your life. A tendency to rush into things can lead to carelessness, however, and your blatant disregard for personal safety often alarms friends and family! You're not the most reliable of people either, as you're often too busy with the next fascination.

A restless edge to your personality leaves others breathless and you often struggle to respect authority. You're not unkind, but for you compassion and empathy are considered a waste of time and you feel these emotions should instead be replaced with action and initiative. Definitely not the tea and sympathy kind!

Your Emotional Needs: Freedom, challenge

Your Emotional Strengths: Optimism, enthusiasm, exuberance

Your Emotional Challenges: Impatience, off-hand nature, carelessness

Working with your Sagittarius Moon: How much of this

description resonates with you? Be honest! If your Sun Sign is very different to Sagittarius, remember that these Moon Sign traits are often not on display except to those who know you best or when you're under pressure. Try these writing prompts on your Lunar Personality page:

- You need intellectual challenge as well as freedom to do your own thing at all times. In what areas of your life do you feel those needs are satisfied? Is there a part of your life where you feel that everything is too easy, too predictable or too restrictive? Why?
- Write about a time when your optimism and enthusiasm inspired others or when you managed to remain hopeful in a situation that others found depressing and demotivating. How did that make you feel? Were others around you surprised by your actions?
- Think about a time when your impatience was a problem or about a situation where you hurt someone else with your brisk, no-nonsense manner. How did it turn out? How did you feel afterwards?

Moon in Capricorn

Very outwardly calm and even perhaps a little aloof, your instinctive emotional responses are kept well under control. Because you don't like to give away very much about yourself, you enjoy solitude and being self-sufficient. You dislike drama and will do whatever you can to avoid emotional outbursts too. Extremely ambitious, you have an innate need to prove yourself to yourself and to others, and will spend a great deal of time and emotional energy on your goals and objectives.

Capricorn energy is quite serious and sober, and you do have a tendency to moan or to disapprove of other people's more exuberant displays. This is softened by your delightfully dry and self-deprecating wit, however, and those who know you well will testify that you are anything but dull – you just choose not to make a fool of yourself in public!

A strong element of practical common sense underpins your decisions and actions and you are not one to take unnecessary risks. Patience, determination and a cool head in a crisis mark you out as a solid, dependable friend – the type of person we all rely on when things go pear shaped!

Your Emotional Needs: Solitude, composure

Your Emotional Strengths: Practicality, level-headedness, determination

Your Emotional Challenges: Aloofness, withdrawal

Working with your Capricorn Moon: How much of this description resonates with you? Be honest! If your Sun Sign is very different to Capricorn, remember that these Moon Sign traits are often not on display except to those who know you best or when you're under pressure. Try these writing prompts on your Lunar Personality page:

- You need solitude and the feeling that you are in control emotionally in order to feel secure and content. In what areas of your life do you feel those needs are satisfied? Is there a part of your life where you feel forced to socialise more than you would like or where things are out of your hands? Why?
- Write about a time when your level-headed approach to a crisis helped others or recall a goal which you focused on with determination and care. How did that make you feel? Were others around you surprised by your actions?
- Think about a time when you have found it difficult to connect with others emotionally or when you have found a social situation uncomfortable. How did it turn out? How did you feel afterwards?

Moon in Aquarius

Known by your friends as quirky, you have a unique take on life and a wisdom way beyond your years. Freedom is very important with this placing and you won't take kindly to being told what to do or – even less – what to think. A broad-minded attitude appeals to others because you don't judge people, but you do maintain a certain amount of emotional distance from even your closest friends.

Aquarian energy is detached and rational, so you tend to find yourself overanalysing your emotions and wondering how you're supposed to feel. You like to surprise others and can be highly unpredictable, often deliberately so. With bright ideas and a stroke of weird genius, you're always up for the latest in technology and are easily enthralled by anything fresh and modern.

One of the zodiac's true humanitarians, your emotions are deeply stirred by injustice and inequality and you can bring tremendous passion and insight to controversial subjects. Because of your unshakeable belief that you are right, however, you can find yourself in hot water with authority figures and have been known to break the rules just for the sake of breaking the rules!

Your Emotional Needs: Independence, justice

Your Emotional Strengths: Logic, originality

Your Emotional Challenges: Unpredictability, distance

Working with your Aquarius Moon: How much of this description resonates with you? Be honest! If your Sun Sign is very different to Aquarius, remember that these Moon Sign traits are often not on display except to those who know you best or when you're under pressure. Try these writing prompts on your Lunar Personality page:

- You need independence as well as the knowledge that situations are fair and just. In what areas of your life do you feel those needs are satisfied? Is there a part of your life where you feel that your actions are too restricted or a situation which you believe is profoundly unfair? Why?

- Write about a time when you used logic to find your way through a difficult challenge, or where your originality shone through and turned an everyday task into something unique. How did that make you feel? Were others around you surprised by your actions?
- Think about a time when you've done something others weren't expecting you to do, perhaps even though you knew it wasn't for the best. Was there a time when you couldn't help keeping your emotional distance from someone even though you wanted to be closer to them? How did it turn out? How did you feel afterwards?

Moon in Pisces

The undisputed romantic of the zodiac, you're a sensitive, intuitive and highly emotional person and you wear your heart on your sleeve for all to see. Easily moved both to laughter and to tears, you are quick to respond to other's emotional needs or to give to charitable causes. Sacrificing your own desires in order to help others is a very strong part of your character.

Creative and dreamy, your imagination soars and you may choose to take refuge in make-believe worlds when life is just too draining or depressing for you. Not always as honest as you might be, your dishonesty is nonetheless usually for the best of motives – blurring the line between fantasy and reality can lead you into trouble, however.

Deeply empathetic and kind, you soak up the emotions of others like a sponge, so being around negative people for extended periods of time can be quite damaging to you. Trusting your instincts isn't always easy for you but they very rarely let you down. Conversely, you find logic tricky and will often act against what seems to be the most sensible option at the time.

Your Emotional Needs: Escapism, creative outlet

Your Emotional Strengths: Compassion, imagination, sacrifice

Your Emotional Challenges: Dishonesty, muddled thinking

Working with your Pisces Moon: How much of this description resonates with you? Be honest! If your Sun Sign is very different to Pisces, remember that these Moon Sign traits are often not on display except to those who know you best or when you're under pressure. Try these writing prompts on your Lunar Personality page:

- You need a certain amount of escapism and creativity in your life in order to lessen the pressures on your sensitive nature. In what areas of your life do you feel those needs are satisfied? Is there a part of your life where you feel that your creativity is stifled or that you have no escape from a grinding reality? Why?
- Write about a time when you didn't mind sacrificing something in order to help someone else, or a time when your compassion saw through someone's rough exterior to the troubled person beneath. How did that make you feel? Were others around you surprised by your actions?
- Think about a time when your dishonesty was a problem or when you became overly muddled and confused about how to handle a difficult situation. How did it turn out? How did you feel afterwards?

Your Moon~Sun Combination: Balancing Energies

In astrology, the Sun represents the ego; the Sun Sign shows how you perceive yourself – what you see when you look in the mirror. To a certain extent, the Sun also represents the image you present to others, although the Ascendant Sign also influences how others see you. It is the Moon which represents your true self, the inner you – the one only your closest friends and family will recognise and which you may only grudgingly acknowledge.

If there is a conflict between the energies of your Sun Sign and those of your Moon Sign, this can lead to inner turmoil or an internal tug of war, especially when it comes to dealing with your emotions. If the two sets of energies complement one another then your emotional life will be a much smoother ride, but you will perhaps miss out on some deeply moving and life-changing experiences.

A complete analysis of all 144 Sun-Moon combinations is beyond the scope of this book, but a basic overview of how these two energies work together will be useful for you to bear in mind. There is space on your Lunar Personality page to record your initial thoughts about your Sun-Moon combination. As you read the summary below, think about how they apply to your own personal circumstances and personality.

Quick Reference Sign Elements

Fire Signs: Aries, Leo, Sagittarius
Earth Signs: Taurus, Virgo, Capricorn
Air Signs: Gemini, Libra, Aquarius
Water Signs: Cancer, Scorpio, Pisces

Fire Sun with Fire Moon – extremely hot-headed, impulsive and dramatic, this is a fiery combination and indicates someone who lives by their wits.

Fire Sun with Earth Moon – the placid, sensible Moon is energised and invigorated by the Sun, but too much risk-taking can leave you feeling ill and out of control.

Fire Sun with Air Moon – an intelligent and dynamic combination with many leadership qualities, but a tendency to overanalyse emotions hampers your instincts.

Fire Sun with Water Moon – this sensitive Moon shies away from the all-action Sun attitude, leaving you torn between two extremes.

Earth Sun with Fire Moon – prone to emotional outbursts at

inopportune moments, you suppress your wilder instincts well but that leaves you wondering about missed opportunities.

Earth Sun with Earth Moon – you're very stable, dependable and warm but you struggle to move forward in life and have a knack for doing things the hard way.

Earth Sun with Air Moon – intelligent and capable, you have big dreams and the tenacity to achieve them, but emotions are tucked away and labelled as an inconvenience.

Earth Sun and Water Moon – still waters run deep with this combination; beneath a placid exterior you are a whirlpool of feelings which you struggle to express.

Air Sun with Fire Moon – the typical head versus heart conflict goes on here. You have both logic and intuition in abundance, but they rarely agree with one another!

Air Sun with Earth Moon – your gentle Moon sometimes struggles with the lively, sociable Sun energies, leading to a lack of confidence despite your intelligence and common sense.

Air Sun with Air Moon – lively, communicative and sociable, this combination is all about ideas, but does tend to flounder in emotional situations when the right words simply cannot be found.

Air Sun with Water Moon – the friendly Sun masks some very deep-seated emotions; you often find yourself agreeing to someone's face but loathing them behind the scenes.

Water Sun with Fire Moon – Creative, imaginative and driven, but sometimes driven to extremes in pursuit of wildly fluctuating desires and emotions.

Water Sun with Earth Moon – the stable, sensible Moon energies successfully calm the Sun's worst fears, giving a balanced combination making good use of both head and heart.

Water Sun with Air Moon – a potent combination of imagination and worry, this can be a stressful mix as the emotional Sun whips the Moon's airy thoughts into a frenzy.

Water Sun with Water Moon – extremely emotional, sensitive

and complex, this is a heart-on-sleeve combination, open to both great heights and frightening depths.

Exercise: Your Moon and Sun

- Think about the basic qualities shown by your Sun Sign (check any astrology book or website if you're not familiar with these) and the ones typical of your Moon Sign. Make a list of the two different types of energies. How do these apply to your personality? Can you think of a time when your head ruled your heart, or the other way round? Are these energies largely complementary or often at odds with one another? Can you feel them at work?
- How does the person you see in the mirror differ from the person your closest friends and family would describe? Can you identify your Sun Sign in one and your Moon Sign in the other?
- Think of a moment of stress or conflict in your life when you used the qualities of your Sun Sign to deal with things. Were you acting the way you expected yourself to act? Did you surprise yourself? Think of another moment when you reacted in a way more like your Moon Sign. How did that feel? More or less "you" than the first moment you described?
- If both your Sun and Moon share the same element (both fire signs, both earth, both air or both water), can you spot the subtle differences between the way you are in the mirror (your ego) and the way you are deep inside? This is harder to see if both signs are in the same element, but the differences are still there.
- If both your Sun and Moon share the same sign, your traits of that sign will be very dominant in your personality. In some ways, you are fortunate, because there should be little or no conflict between your ego and your inner self. The person in the mirror reacts exactly the way the real

you does. On the other hand, you may feel the lack of input from another element. Think of a time when you felt that your overabundance of earth, air, fire or water hindered you in making the right choice or dealing appropriately with a situation. Which of the other elements might have helped?

By now you should be getting a good idea of the properties of your Moon Sign and how they are expressed. In the next chapter, we're going to move on to look at whereabouts in the birth chart wheel the Moon was when you were born, and which area of life the Moon's energies focus on for you.

Chapter 2

Your Lunar Focus

Now you know how the Moon expresses its energies via your Moon Sign, but did you know that the position of the Moon in your natal chart also highlights a focus on a particular area of your life? Let's find out what house your Moon is in and what that might mean for you.

What is a House?

Astrologers divide the heavens – and therefore your astrological chart wheel – into twelve different sections, called houses. Each house represents a different part of your life – family, love, school, friends and so on. There are many varied ways of calculating these twelve divisions, but for the purpose of this book we're going to use a method called the Equal House system, which simply divides the chart wheel into twelve equal slices. Figure 1 illustrates what the different slices of the wheel represent.

1 = image, self-esteem
2 = security and money
3 = school, communication, intellect
4 = home, parents, family
5 = hobbies, risks, creativity
6 = health, exercise, routine matters
7 = love and relationships
8 = karma, mysteries, obligations
9 = travel, dreams, spirituality
10 = status and ambitions
11 = friends and social conscience
12 = privacy, fears, intuition

Astrological Houses and their Focus Areas

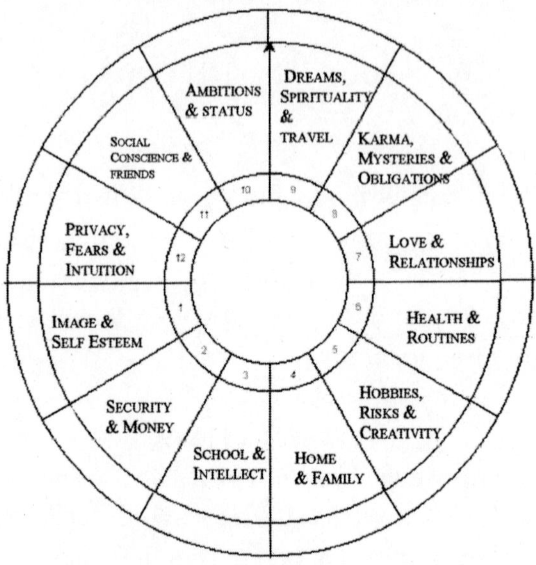

Figure 1

In order to slice up the chart, you need to know where your Ascendant falls. The Ascendant is the sign which was rising in the East at the time and place of your birth. Remember when you looked up your Moon Sign? It's that little piece of information which said Ascendant Scorpio 17.34/AC Scorpio 17 34/Rising Sign 17 degrees Scorpio (obviously your own sign/numbers will be different) which you need now. The Ascendant is a very important astrological factor in its own right, so you might like to take a few moments to look up an interpretation of its qualities – googling Virgo Ascendant, for instance, will give you lots of information.

Dividing Your Chart into Houses

Don't worry, this isn't as complicated as you might think – but there are a few things you need to understand first. Have a look at Figure 2. A chart wheel before someone's birth data is calculated is always shown with the Ascendant being 0º Aries, which you can see here marked at the 9 o'clock position on the wheel. Once your own Ascendant is shown, the sign and degree here will be different, but it will **always be marked at the same 9 o'clock position**. On the chart wheel, you can also see the zodiac signs listed in their correct order, beginning with Aries and ending with Pisces, going anticlockwise around the wheel. **The signs will always stay in the same order, although the sign at the starting point (9 o'clock) will change in each individual chart.** Gemini will always follow Taurus, which will always follow Aries, and so on.

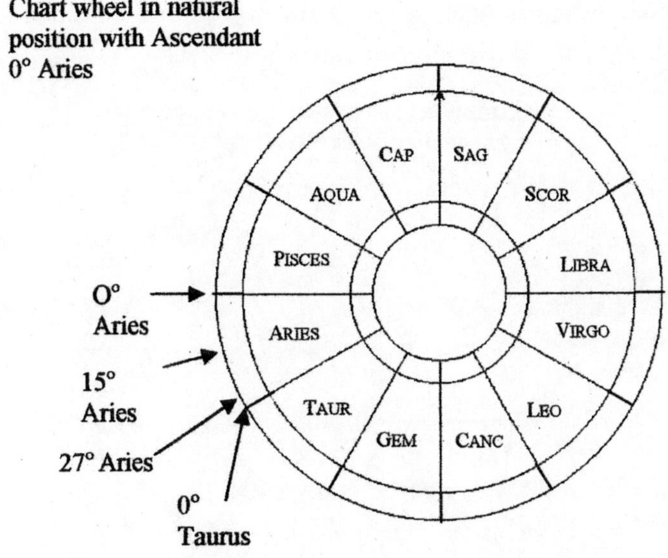

Figure 2

If you remember your maths, you'll know that a circle contains 360º – so it follows that if we are dividing it into twelve slices, each slice, or house, will occupy 30º of the circle. To illustrate this, you can see on Figure 2 that a position of 15º Aries is about halfway along the Aries slice, while 27º Aries is nearly at the cusp with Taurus. Once the sign changes, we go back to 0° again and work our way up to 30° of that sign. **The Ascendant always marks the cusp of the 1st House, so the cusp of the 2nd House is always 30° along from the 1st, then the 3rd is 30° along from the 2nd, etc.**

Now, imagine Figure 2 superimposed on top of Figure 1. You can see that the cusps between the signs and the cusps between the houses match up exactly, and Aries covers all of the 1st House, Taurus covers all of the 2nd House and so on.

So far, so good. But your Ascendant is highly unlikely to be 0° Aries. When we put your Ascendant on the chart, we have to twist the wheel so that your Ascendant is at the 9 o'clock position, because, remember, that's where the Ascendant is always shown. Have a look at Figure 3.

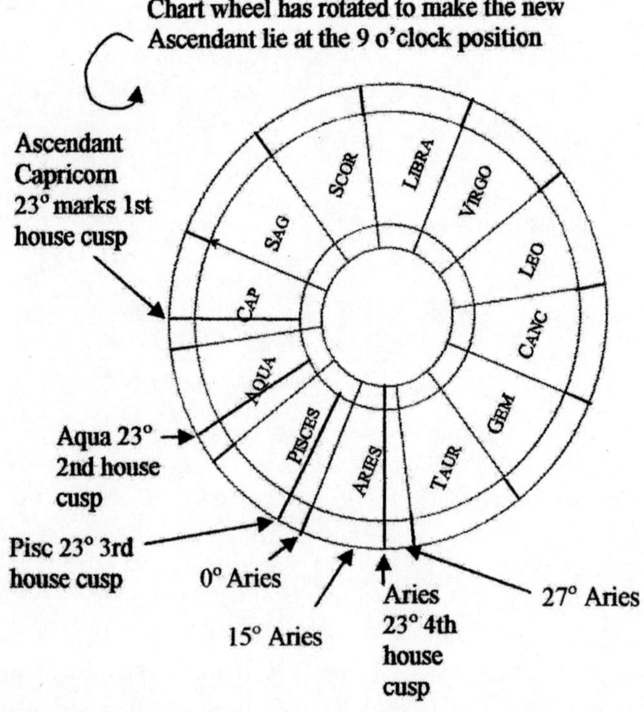

Figure 3

Figure 3 shows Figure 2 rotated for someone with an Ascendant of 23° Capricorn. Because that Ascendant now marks the cusp of the 1st House, the 2nd House begins at 23° Aquarius, the 3rd House begins at 23° Pisces and so on around the wheel. You can see now that the 1st House in this chart is occupied by a little bit of Capricorn and a lot of Aquarius – it's important to understand that **very often, two signs "share" a house, because of the position of the Ascendant.** Note that while in Figure 2, the 0°, 15° and 27° Aries points were all within the 1st House. In Figure 3, the 0° and 15° Aries are in the 3rd House, while the 27° Aries is in the 4th House.

Don't panic! This might all seem very hard to grasp at first, but it's very simple when you get used to the idea. Use the explanations above and the diagrams to help you as we walk step by step through the process of finding out which house your Moon is in. I'm going to work with an example of an Ascendant at 22° Virgo and a Moon at 4° Aries, but of course you should use your own figures.

Blank Birth Chart Wheel

Use this wheel to fill in your Ascendant, House Cusps and Moon position

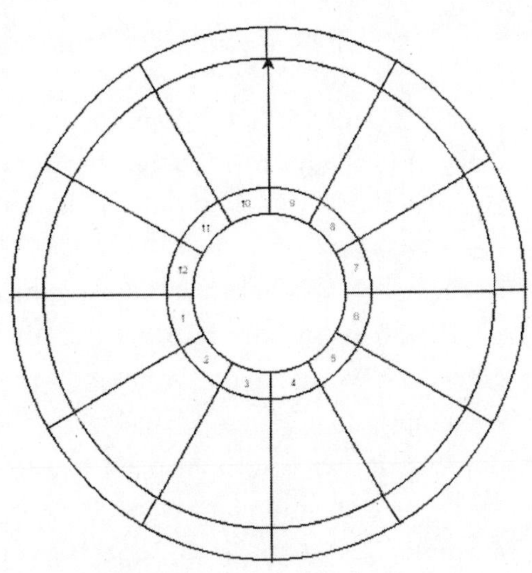

Figure 4

1 Start with a blank chart wheel. You can use the one shown in Figure 4, download one from the website, or you'll find many printable blank ones on the Internet.

2 Find the ready drawn line at the 9 o'clock position on the chart wheel. This is the Ascendant line. Next to that line, outside the chart, write the Ascendant data you were given, eg 22 Virgo. This line now represents 22° of Virgo. The second figure, if you were given data in a format like Ascendant Virgo 22.14, is "minutes", but you don't need to worry about those; the degrees figure will give you all the accuracy you need.

3 Remember that each little slice of the wheel is 30° and each zodiac sign also covers 30° of the chart. It follows that the next line around the wheel, in an anticlockwise direction (think 8 o'clock), will be 22° Libra. Next (think 7 o'clock) will be 22° Scorpio. Carry on labelling each line, all the way around, until you reach the 10 o'clock position, which in my example would be labelled 22° Leo – see Figure 5.

4 OK, so now we know where all the house divisions fall, but which house is which? That one's simple, and is the same on every chart. The slice between the Ascendant line and the next anticlockwise line (between 9 o'clock and 8 o'clock) is always the first house. The house numbers are already filled in for you on the blank chart, because they never change.

5 Lastly, let's find out which house your natal Moon was in when you were born. Go back to the figures you were given for your Moon Sign and you'll find they say something like Aries 4.20. Again, the first figure, the degrees figure, is all you need to worry about. Can you spot where on your chart wheel the Moon would be? In my example, 22° Aries is the line between the 7th and 8th Houses. The red dotted line shows the approximate space covered by the whole 30° of Aries, with anything between

22° and 30° being in the 8th House, whereas anything between 0° and 21° would be in the 7th House. The Moon in my example at 4° Aries would lie in the 7th House. If it had been, say, 26° Aries, it would have been in the 8th House. Find your Moon and draw a little Moon symbol in the correct house. You're done!

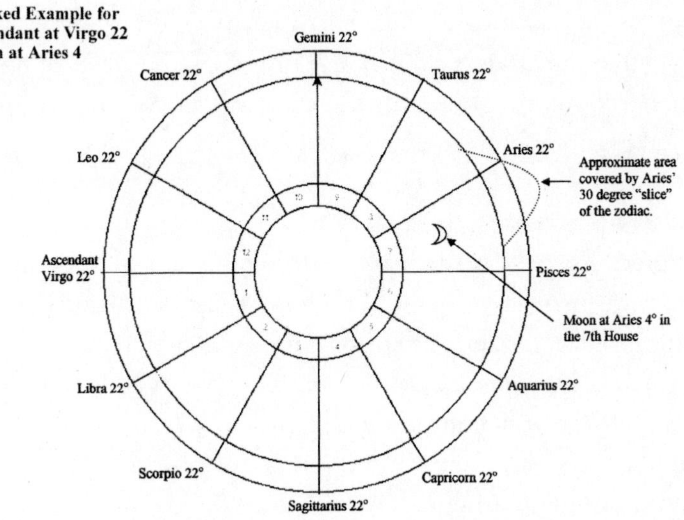

Figure 5

Take a moment to start filling in your Lunar Focus page – you can make one for yourself or download one from the website. Fill in which house the Moon was occupying when you were born and note down your initial thoughts about this. Are you conscious of the affairs of that house weighing on your mind a great deal? Or is your Moon working at a deeper, more subconscious level in this area?

The Moon Through the Houses

The Moon orbits around the Earth constantly, taking approximately 28 days to complete one orbit, spending just over 2 days in each zodiac sign. In any given month, the Moon will have travelled right around your chart wheel, spending some time in every sign and every house. This monthly journey is an enormously important part of lunar astrology, and we'll look at it in-depth in the next chapter. For now, let's look at the significance of which house the Moon occupied when you were born.

The area of life indicated by your Moon House will be of special importance to you, particularly on an emotional level. Whether the affairs of this house promote your deepest passions or harbour your darkest fears, they will be an inescapable and vital part of who you are.

Moon in 1st House

Protection, both of yourself and of others, is a key emotional driving force in your life. You have a gentle, nurturing disposition, a very strong intuition and your actions are governed primarily by your emotions rather than by rational thought. Your relationship with your mum is a particular focus in your life and the bond between the two of you is exceptionally strong, albeit periodically tumultuous. Worry and emotional turmoil can affect your health, particularly your skin. Have you noticed how your spots get worse when you're going through a tense few days?

1st House Challenge: Getting the balance of emotional expression right – you tend to either repress your emotions or let them flood out at inappropriate moments.

Working with your 1st House Moon

Try one or more of these journal prompts to explore how your 1st House Moon is at work in your life.

- Refer to your Moon Sign strengths, weaknesses and challenges. How do these relate to the 1st House? Do you think the energies of your Moon Sign work well in this house, or is there friction between the energies of the sign and those of the house? Example: the Gemini Moon is very rational and logical and tends to struggle with the deeply held emotions of the 1st House. A struggle between the head and the heart would be evident with those placings. By contrast, the Cancer Moon is emotional and nurturing and "fits" easily with the 1st House need to protect. These placings would enhance your sensitivity and place your family very firmly at the heart of your priorities.

- When was the last time you thought a problem through, step by step, instead of impulsively following your heart? Can you think of a time when that would have helped you, or a time when you did just that but would have been better off following your instincts?
- Do you tend to bottle up your emotions only to explode later? How can you use the energies of your Moon Sign to help you meet the 1st House Challenge of more balanced emotional expression?

Moon in 2nd House

A need for emotional and financial security underpins your life's motivations. You dislike the unknown and often take steps to plan ahead in great detail, but in doing so you miss out on some of life's spontaneity. You tend to hoard items of sentimental value and you're relatively materialistic by instinct – although you may well be generous or reckless in your spending and giving, there is always a basic need to "acquire" working in the background. Jealousy and possessiveness can be issues for you as you feel that others should belong to you in the same way as your possessions do.

2nd House Challenge: Balancing security and risk, safety and adventure – what is your need to be emotionally safe costing you in the long run?

Working with your 2nd House Moon

Try one or more of these journal prompts to explore how your 2nd House Moon is at work in your life.

- Refer to your Moon Sign strengths, weaknesses and challenges. How do these relate to the 2nd House? Do you think the energies of your Moon Sign work well in this house, or is there friction between the energies of the sign and those of the house? Example: the Capricorn Moon is level-headed, practical and resourceful and works well with the 2nd House need for security, but these placings could lead to an overly rigid approach to life. By contrast, the Aries Moon has a reckless edge and a pioneering spirit and would struggle slightly with a 2nd House placing, leading to bouts of overspending or spontaneity that later cause guilt or anxiety.
- Can you recall a time when you felt anxious, betrayed or angry over a loved one's actions because of jealousy or possessiveness? Looking back, do you think your feelings were justified?
- Do you tend to fluctuate between impulsiveness and caution? How can you use the energies of your Moon Sign to help you meet the 2nd House Challenge of a more balanced approach to security?

Moon in 3rd House

Chatterbox! You have an instinctive need to communicate – as much and as often as possible, by any means! Education comes easily to you, but you tend to have a little knowledge of lots of subjects rather than an in-depth focus on any one thing. It's easy for you to put your feelings into words, but you're not always tactful and your direct approach is not to everyone's taste. Brothers and sisters – or the lack of them – figure strongly in your life and you like to be surrounded by people. A consummate spin doctor, your intellect can be both your greatest asset and the biggest barrier between you and the relationships you seek.

3rd House Challenge: Focus – you bore easily and it's often hard for you to find the staying power you need to make real progress towards your goals.

Working with your 3rd House Moon

Try one or more of these journal prompts to explore how your 3rd House Moon is at work in your life.

- Refer to your Moon Sign strengths, weaknesses and challenges. How do these relate to the 3rd House? Do you think the energies of your Moon Sign work well in this house, or is there friction between the energies of the sign and those of the house? Example: the Virgo Moon is reticent and sometimes a little shy; combined with the energies of the 3rd House, this could lead to an internal battle and someone who would love to be more socially involved but can't quite figure out how. By contrast, the socially at ease Libra Moon blends well with the 3rd House energies but may result in an overly superficial personality or someone who merely says what others want to hear.
- Can you recall a time when being alone made you feel anxious or left out? Are you at ease with your own company or do you feel the need to chatter and constantly fill in empty spaces?
- Do you tend to rush through tasks without giving them your all? How can you use the energies of your Moon Sign to help you meet the 3rd House Challenge of greater focus?

Moon in 4th House

Family ties are the most fundamentally important part of your emotional well-being. You pick up on the mood at home very easily and can be instantly elated or depressed depending what's going on there. You're emotionally drawn to the past and enjoy finding out about your family history, but a desire to live in the past can lead to introversion, sulkiness and a fear of the future. With exceptionally strong maternal instincts, you are drawn to young children and could not imagine not having a family of your own in due course.

4th House Challenge: Confidence and self-identity – it's not easy for you to see yourself as an individual, separate from your family although loved and nurtured.

Working with your 4th House Moon

Try one or more of these journal prompts to explore how your 4th House Moon is at work in your life.

- Refer to your Moon Sign strengths, weaknesses and challenges. How do these relate to the 4th House? Do you think the energies of your Moon Sign work well in this house, or is there friction between the energies of the sign and those of the house? Example: the Aquarius Moon needs freedom and independence and could find the 4th House need for family ties restrictive or suffocating, leading to periods of distance and isolation. By contrast, the stable and sensible Taurus Moon blends well with 4th House energies and has the common sense and determination to overcome any lack of confidence.
- Can you recall a time when you have used your family "identity" to excuse the way things are or as an excuse for not doing something you didn't really want to do anyway? What about a time when you wished for more independence and to do things your own way? How did that turn out?
- Do you tend to lack confidence? How can you use the energies of your Moon Sign to help you meet the 4th House Challenge of greater self-identity?

Moon in 5th House

You have an instinctive need to be creative, whether that's through art, crafts, music, words or simply a fertile imagination. Your playful emotional nature is youthful and often charming, but you tend to move from one extreme to the other – from overconfidence to reticence and back again with alarming speed. There's also an emotional need to take risks. Sometimes reckless, especially in love and with money, you consistently push at the boundaries of your luck and talents to see how far you can go and where it will all lead. In many ways an eternal child, you're adept at filling your time with hobbies and passions.

5th House Challenge: Restraint – by constantly creating dramas and going to extremes, you waste a great deal of emotional energy and personal potential.

Working with your 5th House Moon

Try one or more of these journal prompts to explore how your 5th House Moon is at work in your life.

- Refer to your Moon Sign strengths, weaknesses and challenges. How do these relate to the 5th House? Do you think the energies of your Moon Sign work well in this house, or is there friction between the energies of the sign and those of the house? Example: the Sagittarius Moon is exuberant, impatient and restless. Combined with the risk-taking energies of the 5th House, this could lead to serial drama and upheaval in life with little respite. By contrast, the gentle and spiritual Pisces Moon could calm the 5th House recklessness and, if channelled well, this combination could promote exceptional artistic talents.
- Can you recall a time when you deliberately or unconsciously took something to extremes? What were you hoping to achieve, or were you so caught up in the experience that you didn't realise how you were behaving

until afterwards?

- Do you tend to manufacture dramas around yourself in order to gain attention or stave off boredom? How can you use the energies of your Moon Sign to help you meet the 5th House Challenge of greater restraint?

Moon in 6th House

Your physical and emotional health are inextricably linked, and upheaval in one will affect the other. With a fundamental emotional need for routine and habit, you have quite an addictive personality and you find it difficult to give up something, even when you know it is for the best – in this way, you can be rather contrary. You have a very strong work ethic and an instinctive need to serve others, to be helpful and to contribute to society. You also, however, have a very loud and persistent inner critic and you struggle emotionally with the feeling that you're not being the best you can be or are not good enough.

6th House Challenge: Spontaneity – because you rely on routines for a sense of security, it's difficult for you to embrace the unknown or to go off on a whim.

Working with your 6th House Moon

Try one or more of these journal prompts to explore how your 6th House Moon is at work in your life.

- Refer to your Moon Sign strengths, weaknesses and challenges. How do these relate to the 6th House? Do you think the energies of your Moon Sign work well in this house, or is there friction between the energies of the sign and those of the house? Example: the dramatic energies of the Leo Moon need the kind of spontaneity and exuberance that the 6th House just doesn't provide. With this combination, you might feel trapped by your daily life. The intense and focused Scorpio Moon energies, on the other hand, blend well with the steadiness of the 6th House and with this placement you might become extraordinarily skilled at what you do.

- Can you recall a time when you have become ill because of emotional stress or, vice versa, where being physically unwell has caused you great emotional upset or a descent into depression? What about those moments when you feel on top of the world? Have you noticed your emotional and physical health being in sync?
- Do you tend to shun the unexpected and cling to your routines? How can you use the energies of your Moon Sign to help you meet the 6th House Challenge of greater spontaneity?

Moon in 7th House

An instinctive need for a close partnership underpins everything you do. You don't quite feel complete when you're single and you're most definitely in love with the idea of love. It's all too easy for you to see yourself as half of a duo rather than as a person in your own right and this can cause self-identity wobbles and insecurities. Loneliness is a physical pain for you, even as a child, but your neediness can drive others away. Faithful, loyal and honest, you expect high standards from everyone around you and this way you can be an inspiration and a driving force to help someone else improve themselves.

7th House Challenge: Independence – your fear of being alone or single leads you into relationships and situations you would be better off avoiding.

Working with your 7th House Moon

Try one or more of these journal prompts to explore how your 7th House Moon is at work in your life.

- Refer to your Moon Sign strengths, weaknesses and

challenges. How do these relate to the 7th House? Do you think the energies of your Moon Sign work well in this house, or is there friction between the energies of the sign and those of the house? Example: the Aquarius Moon has a breezy, independent nature which helps to alleviate the 7th House tendency to be over-dependent upon a partner. The Libra Moon, on the other hand, goes to great lengths to avoid discord; blended with the 7th House need for a relationship, this could lead to great inertia and the inability to recognise when someone is not good for you.

- Can you recall a time when you have felt upset or taken it too personally when friends or a boyfriend have not been available to spend time with you? Do you think you find it uncomfortable to be alone? What is it about your own company that you find difficult?
- Do you tend to fear striking out on your own? How can you use the energies of your Moon Sign to help you meet the 7th House Challenge of greater independence?

Moon in 8th House

Deep, intense and complex emotions abound here, and even you may not fully understand how you feel a lot of the time. You act according to your instincts, not logic and have a "feel" for what's right and what's wrong. Psychic abilities are strong and you have an interest in the occult, the mysterious and the meaning of life. You don't do anything by halves, and that includes feeling both love and hate, and bearing grudges for a very long time. Jealousy and possessiveness can cause problems, as can deep-seated resentment over your obligations to other people.

8th House Challenge: Trust – you are naturally suspicious of others, but failing to trust can lead to unhappiness and isolation if others resent your suspicions.

Working with your 8th House Moon

Try one or more of these journal prompts to explore how your 8th House Moon is at work in your life.

- Refer to your Moon Sign strengths, weaknesses and challenges. How do these relate to the 8th House? Do you think the energies of your Moon Sign work well in this house, or is there friction between the energies of the sign and those of the house? Example: the gregarious and larger than life energies of the Leo Moon are buoyant enough to withstand 8th House jealousies and big-hearted enough to avoid resentment. Pisces Moon energy is so fragile and easily hurt, however, that a single bad experience, blended with 8th House suspicions, could lead to introversion and an unwillingness to relate to others.
- Can you recall a time when you felt very jealous or envious? How did this affect your life and how did you overcome it in end? Have you experienced someone distrusting you without good reason? How did that make you feel?
- Do you find it hard to trust other people? How can you use the energies of your Moon Sign to help you meet the 8th House Challenge of greater trust?

Moon in 9th House

Your emotions and intellect are very closely tied together and you feel an instinctive need to gather knowledge, to study and to stretch your mind. An eternal scholar and philosopher, you have a strong moral compass but your morals don't necessarily line up with anyone else's. You yearn to travel and can become emotionally restless if you feel stuck in a rut. Becoming too wrapped up in a quest for truth can lead to a life which drifts along – although you have so much potential, a solid, practical, goal orientated push is needed from somewhere in order for you to reach those aims.

9th House Challenge: Practical realisation of ideals – all the abstract thought in the world is no good if you cannot put your ideas into action.

Working with your 9th House Moon

Try one or more of these journal prompts to explore how your 9th House Moon is at work in your life.

- Refer to your Moon Sign strengths, weaknesses and challenges. How do these relate to the 9th House? Do you think the energies of your Moon Sign work well in this house, or is there friction between the energies of the sign and those of the house? Example: the Gemini Moon has an intellectual quality which is very compatible with the 9th House, but could result in all talk, no action and frustrated dreams. By contrast, the solid, practical, can-do energies of the Capricorn Moon blend well with the 9th House idealisms and intelligence – and this combination can get things done.
- Can you recall a time when you have researched a subject just for the pure pleasure of gaining the knowledge? Do you enjoy watching documentaries and listening to the news? Or do you struggle with study and prefer a more hands-on approach?
- Do you tend to have big ideas which don't come to fruition? How can you use the energies of your Moon Sign to help you meet the 9th House Challenge of greater practicality?

Moon in 10th House

Your emotional well-being is very dependent upon how you perceive your status in life and how successful or popular you think you are. In your head, it's all about what others think rather than what you feel. Your relationship with your father is a source of emotional depth for you, either because you are very close, or because you are not. You are very driven and will not rest until you get your way. With exceptional leadership potential and an influence upon others which is more profound than you realise, your very strong ambitions stand every chance of being achieved – but sometimes at personal or emotional cost.

10th House Challenge: Spirituality and peace – learning to be happy with what you have. Discover that there is more to life than money, success or fame.

Working with your 10th House Moon

Try one or more of these journal prompts to explore how your 10th House Moon is at work in your life.

- Refer to your Moon Sign strengths, weaknesses and challenges. How do these relate to the 10th House? Do you think the energies of your Moon Sign work well in this house, or is there friction between the energies of the sign and those of the house? Example: the nurturing and home loving qualities of Cancer don't sit easily with 10th House ambitions; this is a classic combination for the career woman who wishes she could spend more time with her kids. The dynamic, trail-blazing energies of the Aries Moon bring extra pizzazz and fire to the 10th House drive for success, often with amazing results – but at what cost?
- Can you recall a time when you absolutely had to win, come first or be the best at something, no matter what? Did you succeed? What did you miss out on in order to do that? How about a time when you didn't bother to do your best. How did that make you feel?
- Do you tend to pay too much attention to wealth or status, both yours and that of others? How can you use the energies of your Moon Sign to help you meet the 10th House Challenge of greater spirituality or peace?

Moon in 11th House

Your emotional intensity is directed towards friends, humanitarian causes and the greater good of society, rather than towards your own family or a love relationship. Gregarious but aloof at the same time, you walk a difficult tight rope between wanting to be loved by others and wanting to maintain your privacy. Surrounded by friends you are indeed, most of the time, but you don't necessarily have a very deep bond with most of them. Relationships can be quite superficial, but you do feel passionate about improving the world and will form strong alliances with others who feel the same.

11th House Challenge: Emotional depth and commitment – it's not easy for you to allow others to get close enough to know the real you.

Working with your 11th House Moon

Try one or more of these journal prompts to explore how your 11th House Moon is at work in your life.

- Refer to your Moon Sign strengths, weaknesses and challenges. How do these relate to the 11th House? Do you think the energies of your Moon Sign work well in this house, or is there friction between the energies of the sign and those of the house? Example: the extremely deep emotional energies of Scorpio would sit ill at ease with the cool and aloof 11th House mode of operating; with this combination, you might find it hard to express how you feel. The Taurus Moon's warmth and humour, on the other hand, exploits the best of the 11th House gregariousness while minimising the detached and overly private energies.
- Can you recall a time when you have worked with a group of others for charity or a selfless purpose? Did you enjoy it and form some good friendships from the experience, or

did you not want to keep in touch with others once they'd served their purpose?

- Do you tend to allow people into your life only so far and no further? How can you use the energies of your Moon Sign to help you meet the 11th House Challenge of emotional depth and commitment?

Moon in 12th House

Your strongest emotional need is for peace and quiet – not all the time, but often and regularly. You like your own company and you sometimes find the hustle bustle of life just a little bit too much. Extremely kind, sympathetic and intuitive, you are a gentle and supportive friend, but you do tend to daydream your life away and to have an overly romantic, unrealistic expectation of love. Secretive and sometimes a little bit of a martyr, you don't spend a lot of time talking about your feelings. Self-sacrifice is a key issue here too and you are often to be found as the quiet, unassuming, back room heroine.

12th House Challenge: Honesty – sometimes lying is the easy option, but it can become a habit. Honesty and realism with yourself is just as important.

Working with your 12th House Moon

Try one or more of these journal prompts to explore how your 12th House Moon is at work in your life.

- Refer to your Moon Sign strengths, weaknesses and challenges. How do these relate to the 12th House? Do you think the energies of your Moon Sign work well in this house, or is there friction between the energies of the sign and those of the house? Example: the bold and brash energies of the Sagittarius Moon are too loud for the sensitive, private 12th House and here there could be a constant struggle between the need for action and the desire for privacy. Quiet and unassuming Virgo Moon energies are a better blend, but with little impetus to face the world this combination could result in a great deal of shyness or low self-esteem.

- Can you recall a time when you have shunned a social event because you simply didn't fancy the noise and the hassle? Were you able to explain your decision to others, or did you feel under pressure to join in? Did you later regret not attending or did you enjoy your quiet time?
- Do you tend to lie to others or view the world through unrealistic, rose-tinted glasses? How can you use the energies of your Moon Sign to help you meet the 12th House Challenge of truth and realism?

Now you know what sign the Moon was in when you were born, and in which house of your natal chart it was. These factors will stay the same throughout your lifetime, but the Moon as seen from Earth moves through all of the zodiac signs every month – and through each one your houses. In the next chapter, we'll find out how to follow that monthly journey and how to make the most of the Moon's changing energies in your life.

Chapter 3

Your Monthly Moon Journey

Seen from the Earth, the Moon is on a continuous journey through the sky and through the zodiac. It takes approximately 28 days for one cycle, with the Moon taking about two and half days to pass through each sign. As you can see from the chart wheel you have been working with, this journey through the zodiac will also take the Moon through each of your 12 astrological houses, bringing sensitive, emotional and intuitive energies into each area of your life in turn.

By tracking this monthly lunar journey, and by knowing which house the Moon is occupying on any given day, you can prepare yourself to work with the Moon's energies, instead of trying to fight against them. It's not much use trying to be brave over a relationship row when the Moon's in your 7th House of partnerships, for instance, but it's an excellent time to build bridges and nurture your family when the Moon's influence is affecting your 4th House.

The astrological word we use to describe the Moon's (or any other planet's) movement around the zodiac is "transit". When the Moon is moving through each house, we say it's transiting the 4th (or whichever) House; remember that term, as we'll be using it quite a bit.

Lunar House Transits vs. Lunar Sign Transits

As you will know from previous chapters, the Moon's influence is felt very differently from one zodiac sign to another. The changing Moon Signs through each month affect each day's energies very subtly – a day when the Moon is in gentle, imaginative Pisces will feel very different to most people than a day when the Moon comes over all ambitious and forthright in Aries. The sign transits give an overall flavour to the day, which is available for anyone to tap into and use. If you want to set up a new, positive habit, say, it would be marvellous to try doing that under a solid Taurus Moon, but not so successful under a reckless Sagittarius Moon.

House transits, on the other hand, are personal to you – the Moon might be transiting Scorpio for all of mankind on a certain day, but it will most likely be transiting a different house in your chart to the charts of your parents, friends and teachers.

As you become more adept with lunar astrology, you will learn to blend the Moon's sign energies and house focus, giving you an invaluable insight into each day's energies and opportunities.

Using a Lunar Calendar

Fortunately, these days there are many free to use online tools and calendars which make tracking the Moon's transits easy. I recommend using the one provided at http://www.lunarium.co.uk/calendar/universal.jsp – but you can use any. Don't be intimidated when you first look at the calendar – you won't need to worry about most of the symbols on it. Let's have a look at how to find out exactly where the Moon is on a particular day.

1 Go to the lunar calendar site.
2 In the drop down boxes, choose January 2013 so you can follow this example, and click "generate calendar".
3 Look at the 1st January 2013. What you're looking for here is a sign of the zodiac – you can safely ignore anything and everything else in the box. You should be able to see that there is the sign for Virgo in the box, and the time 17:34. That means the Moon enters Virgo on that date at 17:34, just gone half past five in the afternoon.
4 Now look at the 2nd January – is there a sign of the zodiac

given in that box? No, there isn't – that means that the Moon is still in Virgo. If the date you are looking up does not have a sign of the zodiac in its box, look backwards a day or two until you do see a sign.

5 Look at the 3rd January – again, the Moon is still in Virgo, and in fact remains there until the 4th January at 01:10 in the morning, when it moves into Libra.

6 That's all there is to it – so now look up the year and month you are currently in, and see where the Moon is today. Found it? Excellent.

Now you've learnt how to find out what sign the Moon is in on any given day, we can easily work out which of your astrological houses it is transiting.

Tracking Lunar House Transits

Once you know what sign the Moon is moving through, it's easy peasy to find out which of your astrological houses it is transiting. Remember in Chapter 2 where you learnt how to plot your natal Moon on the chart wheel? It's exactly the same principle here. Find out where the Moon is for the day in question, and then simply mentally pop it into the chart in the right place, and see which house it is affecting.

Let's have a look back at Figure 5 from Chapter 2 and see where the Moon transits fall for the beginning of January 2013.

1 Generate the lunar calendar for January 2013 as you did above.

2 We've already seen that Moon enters Virgo late on the afternoon of the 1st January. Where is 0° Virgo on the example chart? It's in the 12th House, so for this individual, the Moon is transiting her 12th House on the 1st January.

So far so simple. However, as in most charts, in our example chart Virgo (and every other sign) actually covers parts of two astrological houses. At some point between the 1st January and the 4th (when the Moon enters Libra, as you can see on the calendar), the Moon stops transiting this girl's 12th House and begins to transit her 1st House. How can we tell when that is?

To be completely accurate with that is beyond the scope of this book, but we can make a good guestimate which will do perfectly well for now. The important thing to know depends on the degree of your Ascendant sign:

If your Ascendant degree is between 1° and 10°, the Moon will move to transit the next house within the first 24 hours of its entry into a sign.

If your Ascendant degree is between 11° and 20°, the Moon will move to transit the next house roughly halfway between its entry into one sign and its entry into the next.

If your Ascendant degree is between 21° and 30°, the Moon will move to transit the next house 24 hours before it enters the next sign.

So, back to our example chart:

The Ascendant degree for this chart is 22°, so we can estimate that the Moon will not stop transiting the 12th House until 24 hours before it enters Libra. Let's say it will start transiting the 1st House in the early hours of the 3rd January – yes?

We can then move on to say that when the Moon enters Libra on the 4th January, it will stay transiting the 1st House until about 24 hours before it is due to enter Scorpio on the 6th January. So it will begin to transit the 2nd House at about 6 am on the 5th January. It will then keep transiting the 2nd House until 24 hours before the Moon enters its next sign, Sagittarius, on the 8th January. Think of it as a rolling motion.

Let's look at two more examples.

Imagine a chart with an Ascendant of 5° Taurus. Get a blank

chart if you're finding it hard to visualise, and mark the Ascendant on to it, and mark each house division as 5°. Now, what's happening here on the 1st January 2013 when the Moon enters Virgo? Where is 0° Virgo on this chart? Full marks if you said "4th House". On the 1st January, the Moon is transiting this chart's 4th House. Because the Ascendant degree is between 1 and 10, we know that it will move to transit the next house within 24 hours of its arrival in a sign – so by the early hours of the 2nd January, we know that the Moon will be transiting this chart's 5th House. And we know that it will stay transiting the 5th House right through the point where the Moon enters Libra in the early hours of the 4th January – and then, within 24 hours, it will move on to transit the 6th House.

Now, imagine a chart with an Ascendant of 16° Capricorn. Again, draw it if you like – it all helps to get the concept stuck in your head. Where is 0° Virgo on this chart? Yep, it's in the 8th House. Getting the hang of this? So on the 1st January 2013, the Moon is transiting the 8th House of this chart. Because the Ascendant degree is between 11 and 20, we estimate that the Moon will move to transit the 9th House roughly halfway between its entry into one sign and its entry into the next – in this case, halfway between its entry into Virgo on the 1st January, and its entry into Libra on the 4th. Let's say late evening on the 2nd January, then, that the Moon will begin transiting the 9th House of this chart. It will stay transiting the 9th House past the entry to Libra on the 4th, and will move to transit the 10th House about halfway to the next change of sign, so roughly breakfast time on the 5th January.

Phew!

Once you've done this a few times, it will seem simple. Promise. With a little bit of practice, you'll easily be able to look at the lunar calendar and airily pronounce that on day so and so your Moon will be transiting such and such a house. Which is where you want to be – because having that information to hand is a gold mine in terms of being able to plan your life and deal with daily ups and downs.

Exercise: Getting the Hang of Tracking Lunar Transits

If you're confident with this, you can skip the exercise. If it's all still a bit scary, have a go at working out the following little exercises. I've given the answers too, so if you get them right, you'll know you've sussed it.

a For a chart with an Ascendant at 12° Gemini, what house is the Moon transiting on the 1st January 2013? When, approximately, does it move to transit the next house?
b For a chart with an Ascendant at 26° Sagittarius, what house is the Moon transiting on the afternoon of the 23rd January 2013?
c For a chart with an Ascendant of 7° Pisces, what house is the Moon transiting on the 20th January 2013?
[Answers: a) 3rd House, moving to the 4th House late on the 2nd January; b) 7th House, having moved from the 6th to the 7th some time on the 23rd January; c) 3rd House, having moved from the 2nd House by the early hours of the 20th January.]

So, now you are able to find out which of your natal houses the Moon is transiting on any particular day – but what use is that information? When the Moon makes its monthly journey through the zodiac, the emotional and intuitive Moon energy is directed towards the affairs of that particular house. If you know when the Moon's energies are most likely to affect your health, you can make sure that you get some extra sleep at that time; if you know when the Moon is most likely to affect your home life, you can be prepared to handle any family tensions, or be forewarned to work around a problem instead of confronting it head on. Let's have a look at how the transits of the Moon affect each house.

Moon Transits Through the Houses

Moon Transiting the 1st House

Emotional energy of the Moon affects: Your image and self-esteem

During this transit, you can be quite selfish – it's all about you, what you want, what you think and what you feel. It's easy to become demanding at this time, and those with strong or fire Moons can be (even more!) irritable and short-tempered. Because your self-esteem is fluctuating, you take things very personally under this transit, and may be wounded or upset over things which would not normally bother you that much. It's a time when you wear your heart on your sleeve, and not a very good time to try hiding how you feel. You will react to situations instinctively and without much thought, so you will find yourself more impulsive or reckless than normal. Expect to be more sensitive about your appearance too – a spot or bad hair can literally ruin your entire day. Which is pretty awkward, considering that all that emotional turmoil can play havoc with your skin.

Moon Transiting the 2nd House

Emotional energy of the Moon affects: Your feelings about money and security

How you feel about your stuff – particularly your most prized possessions – comes strongly into focus under this transit. You won't be feeling very generous and you'll be upset if someone takes, breaks or messes with something you own. And it doesn't stop with material possessions – you'll be extremely jealous right now if you feel someone is muscling in on a friendship or relationship too, or even if your dog takes a liking to someone! Your sense of security is intimately bound up with your possessions, in as much as they represent who you are and how you got here, so there is more at stake here than just the latest gadget! The impulsive energies of the Moon can lead to unwise spending now, and if the transiting Moon's sign has a wild streak, it will show in your snap decisions and potentially reckless choices. Fundamentally, however, the 2nd House is a house of stability, and if your natal Moon and/or the transiting Moon are in stable, solid, earth signs, you'll fight to keep the status quo alive.

Moon Transiting the 3rd House

Emotional energy of the Moon affects: Your education, communication skills and intellect

During this transit, you will communicate instinctively – and you might well be communicating more than you intend to, with body language giving you away or saying more than you wanted. The Moon's passion will show itself with extra effort on your part at school, and you'll want to cut through the waffle and get to the heart of the matter in everything. Idle social chitchat and the niceties of polite society will irritate you – you want to say what you mean and mean what you say, and you wish everyone else was doing the same. This can be a restless time, and you'll bore easily, so it's important to try to keep yourself busy. New knowledge and new interests come easily under this transit, and you'll love to talk – if you're normally quiet and shy, this is a wonderful transit for starting conversations and getting to know new people.

Moon Transiting the 4th House

Emotional energy of the Moon affects: Your home and family relationships

This transit is a time for privacy, not performance. Your own four walls will be a sanctuary. Having everything just so at home will help you to feel more at ease, so you might find yourself tidying like mad or rearranging furniture in your bedroom. Relationships within the family are hugely important under this transit and will generally be nurturing and positive. However, the Moon's moodiness can cause problems at home, and you may find yourself caught up in petty squabbles among family members. The 4th House is also the house of the past, and of nostalgia, so you could find yourself focusing on your family tree during this transit, or taking trips down memory lane. Old patterns of behaviour will tend to repeat themselves while the Moon transits the 4th House, so if you get a sense of déjà vu, stop and ask yourself whether you're making the same mistakes, in any area of life, that you've already made once. This transit can help you to see clearly where the past can help you and where it's holding you back.

Moon Transiting the 5th House

Emotional energy of the Moon affects: Your hobbies and creativity, and your willingness to take risks

This delightful lunar transit is usually quite light-hearted and playful. At this time, you'll want to show off your talents, whatever they may be, and you'll be seeking attention. Sometimes, however, the need for attention at all costs can lead to you provoking rows or creating drama just for the sake of it. Relaxation and fun are very high up the agenda and you could struggle with more mundane tasks during this transit. It won't be easy to take matters too seriously, but the laughter and frivolity can be very healing. Your attitude towards risk will be greatly affected during this transit, depending on the sign of the transiting Moon – a cautious sign will hold you back from taking a chance which could have been beneficial, while a more impulsive sign could lead you into trouble if you don't think through the options carefully. Younger siblings and pets are also ruled by this house, so your emotional attachments to these family members will deepen.

Moon Transiting the 6th House

Emotional energy of the Moon affects: Your health and routine matters

Emotional upheaval during this transit can have a dramatic effect on your health. When things are going well, you'll be positively glowing, but if you're stressed out your skin will suffer and you'll find it hard to sleep. It's a hard-working time, a "getting down to business" transit, so your plans should start coming together and you'll find it relatively easy to concentrate and to push projects onwards as you move towards your goals. This house is ruled by Virgo, however, and there's a strong sense of perfection surrounding everything which happens here. You can be your own worst enemy under this transit by becoming overly critical of yourself and by believing that you're failing. Great organisation and a logical mind are the keys to harnessing the most positive aspects of this transit, so write lists, make plans and get your tasks in order – if you do, you can achieve a great deal at this time.

Moon Transiting the 7th House

Emotional energy of the Moon affects: Your attitude towards love and relationships

Intense emotions are likely to flare up in a relationship under this transit, but remember that intense is not necessarily bad – in small doses, a bit of fire does no harm and can be healthy. Relationships are the most important thing in your life during this transit and you'll find it difficult to be objective about them, so expect to react to everything with a greater or lesser degree or hysteria. Well, not really, but you will be much more sensitive than normal. If you are single, this transit could well find you feeling lonely and sorry for yourself, but the key would be to work to turn that into a positive celebration of being independent and free. If you're with a partner, this transit could be full of romance or full of drama, but it should certainly be eventful, either way. The sign of the transiting Moon will have a big impact on how you approach your relationship, and on how you express yourself to your partner.

Moon Transiting the 8th House

Emotional energy of the Moon affects: Your karma, mysteries and obligations

A particularly intense and often unsettling transit, this is a time when everything you thought you knew can be challenged. Trust is sometimes either difficult to come by or given much too freely under this transit, and you may be deliberately provoking others in order to (unconsciously) find out how much they care for you. You want to feel things deeply at this time, and so mundane, ordinary life won't be enough. In order to get the rush of emotions, you could be drawn to odd people, or you might put yourself in situations which you would normally avoid. It's an extremely interesting time for developing psychic awareness, and for learning more about the mysteries of life, but you'll feel disillusioned if you have more questions than answers. Sometimes, we behave so weirdly under this transit that other people wonder what's happened to us – indeed, when the 2–3 days have passed, you might find it hard to believe that you really did or said such and such!

Moon Transiting the 9th House

Emotional energy of the Moon affects: Your dreams, spirituality and travel opportunities

This is a transit when freedom is crucially important: on a personal level, you'll want to push the boundaries of what's allowed, for instance by breaking a rule your parents have set; on a more philosophical level, you'll want to stand out from the crowd by thinking, looking or behaving differently. Restlessness is a key feature at this time, and you'll bore quickly at school and even with your favourite friends and hobbies. This is an excellent time for doing something new in order to lift yourself out a rut. You're also extremely open-minded during this transit, and you may be changing or adapting some of your beliefs and principles. The 9th House also represents justice, where the emotional, instinctive lunar response often is that "it's not fair!" – and sometimes it won't be. Learning to deal with life's injustices is a key lesson from this transit, but you are also encouraged to harness the Moon's imagination and to dream big dreams.

Moon Transiting the 10th House

Emotional energy of the Moon affects: Your status and ambitions

This is a transit when you'll want to see results for all your hard work. Ambitions are high, but any competitiveness in your nature is softened by the nurturing energies of the Moon, making this a fabulous time for teamwork. Over-thinking your public image can cause anxiety just now, and you'll be very concerned about what others think of you – even though they probably haven't even noticed that your lippy's smudged. At school, if you're not getting good enough (in your eyes) marks, you'll fret and worry about how this will affect your future, while managing to feel intensely personally scorned into the bargain. Overreactions are likely to anything which relates to your future prospects or ambitions, and nerves can affect your schoolwork – but on the other hand, adrenaline from minor anxiety can enhance it. Depending on the sign of the transiting Moon, this can be a period of great success.

Moon Transiting the 11th House

Emotional energy of the Moon affects: Your friendships and social conscience

A gregarious and sociable transit, this one. You'll want to mix more widely than you normally do, and you'll enjoy making new friends, talking and discovering shared and common interests in a group. However, the Moon's intense emotions can easily provoke jealousy among friends, especially if there is a new member of the group. You will easily soak up other people's moods under this transit, so it helps to surround yourself with positive people, but of course that's easier said than done. You will be easily moved to tears over global or environmental injustices, and happy to harness your passion to do whatever you can to help. It's important not to spend too much time alone during this transit, as you really do feel an instinctive need to socialise – even if it is the middle of a maths lesson! This is a very objective house, which tends to neutralise some of the Moon's subjectivity, so if your natal Moon is in a highly emotional sign, you will be able to be more logical for these days.

Moon Transiting the 12th House

Emotional energy of the Moon affects: Your privacy, fears and intuition

Secrets and lies abound under this mysterious transit. It's an extremely emotional time, even for those with relatively unemotional natal Moons – those with natal Moons in Pisces, Scorpio or Cancer will find this transit almost unbearably intense, whether they're extremely joyful or extremely sad. You'll want to keep your feelings hidden, but at the same time you need to express them before they drive you mad, so there's a push-pull struggle going on between your head and your heart. An overactive imagination can easily build small fears into huge problems during this transit. During this introverted period, you'll want to spend time alone, or perhaps escaping into a good book and a fictional world, but it can actually be a very positive time for learning more about yourself and for uncovering the truth – if you can handle the truth, that is.

Exercise: Daily Journal Sheet

Now that you are able to find out where the Moon is on any given day, and how it will affect your personal chart, it's a good time to get used to filling in a daily journal sheet. You can download one from the website, if you wish, or it's simple to create your own.

Your page should include a space for the date, and for the

position of the Moon. Note which of your houses the Moon is transiting. Use the rest of the space for your personal notes about how you have experienced the day. How do you feel the Moon has made its presence felt in that particular house?

You can fill in a sheet every day, and that would be ideal – but don't worry if you forget days. Just keep the daily journal when you remember to. Over time, after you have been following the Moon's journey through your chart for a few months, you will start to notice patterns emerging. There's more about spotting patterns in the final chapter of this book. Let's move on now to see how New and Full Moons and eclipses fit into your lunar life.

Chapter 4

Special Moons

As the Moon journeys through each 28-day cycle, it passes through eight different phases: new, waxing crescent, first quarter, waxing gibbous, full, waning gibbous, last quarter and waning crescent. You will have noticed these changes in shape and visibility of the Moon throughout your life, probably without really taking much notice. The most important phases for our lunar astrology purposes are the New Moon and the Full Moon. Eclipses of the Moon and of the Sun are also important, and in this chapter we're going to find out what New Moons, Full Moons and eclipses are, and how you can harness their power.

The New Moon: New Beginnings

A New Moon occurs when the Moon, Earth and Sun line up, with the Moon positioned between the Sun and the Earth. The Sun illuminates the dark side of the Moon, the side facing away from the Earth, so we cannot see the Moon at all during a New Moon.

Although the Moon is dark at this time, the New Moon marks the time when the Moon's disc will begin to grow in size in our skies, so astrologically this is a time of new beginnings, fresh starts, optimism, wishes and initiative. All New Moons will be marked on any lunar calendar you use, often indicated by a filled in black circle, symbolising the Moon's lack of visibility at this moment. There will be at least one New Moon in every calendar month.

You can harness the New Moon's energies by choosing this time to start new and positive habits, undertake a major project, make good changes to your life or be honest with yourself about some home truths.

An easy way to keep track of New Moons and their role in your life is to use a New Moon journal page – you can download one from the website, or make your own. Note the date, and which sign and house the Moon is in, and explore your feelings about how it is impacting your life.

Exercise: New Moon Beginnings

Think about something in your life you would really like to change. Explore the roots of why you want to change it. Why is the current situation making you unhappy or not serving you well? Do you honestly want to change things, or do you just think that you ought to? Visualise, for a moment, that you have the power to wave a wand and change things to the way you want them to be. How will you feel once this is changed? How does your new beginning look? Spend ten minutes writing about your life as if the change has already happened. During the next New Moon, try to act for the day as though the change has already taken place.

New Moon Through the Signs

Each New Moon has a slightly different energy, depending on what sign the Moon is in – and each has a slightly different focus for its energy, depending on what house the Moon is transiting at the time.

In order to best use the New Moon's energy, first consider which sign the Moon is in. All New Moons are ideal for new starts, but the energy's mood and strong points will vary, as will potential pitfalls in the energy. A Gemini New Moon would be perfect for joining a new club, for instance, but if you were to start a major school project under a Gemini New Moon you would need to guard against becoming bored with it too quickly. A tactful Libra New Moon is ideal for turning over a new leaf with siblings, but you should take care not to lie your way out of trouble at that time.

New Moon in Aries – fast moving energy with lots of excitement and initiative... but often a hot temper to match.

New Moon in Taurus – determined, stable energy, with a solid, step by step approach to a task... but a reluctance to try the untried.

New Moon in Gemini – sociable, gregarious energy which is excellent for multitasking... but bores easily.

New Moon in Cancer – nurturing, sensitive energy with a good memory and lots of sympathy... but twinges of possessiveness and defensiveness.

New Moon in Leo – regal, dignified and confident energy which expects to succeed... but which can cause offence with its arrogance.

New Moon in Virgo – hard-working and detail-orientated energy which leaves nothing to chance... but which sometimes lacks inspiration and passion.

New Moon in Libra – tactful, peaceful energy with lots of potential for smoothing things over... but a tendency towards little white lies.

New Moon in Scorpio – passionate, forceful energy which does not take no for an answer... but which can be obsessive and overly secretive.

New Moon in Sagittarius – optimistic and fortunate energy filled with adventurous charisma... but a reckless disregard for others' feelings.

New Moon in Capricorn – logical, ambitious and emotionally cool energy which excels at planning... but struggles with expressing feelings.

New Moon in Aquarius – innovative and inventive energy with an independent streak... but may be ahead of its time.

New Moon in Pisces – compassionate, dreamy energy which can harness the magic of imagination... but is easily squashed and depressed.

The Full Moon: Challenge and Reflection

A Full Moon occurs, just like the New Moon, when the Moon, Earth and Sun line up, but this time the Earth is positioned between the Sun and the Moon. The Sun therefore illuminates the full half of Moon which faces us, so we see it as a bright, full circle or disc.

With the Full Moon dominating the sky, this is the time that marks the completion of a cycle. Full Moon is a time to put the finishing touches to a project and to prepare to move on. From this point on, however, the Moon will appear to shrink in the sky, and this is why the Full Moon symbolically brings us challenges. As a result of our past actions, we now have to face certain questions. At Full Moon, emotions are heightened both for better and for worse. Modern statistics tell us about increases in violent behaviour and accidents during a Full Moon; folklore tells us about werewolves and other mythological creatures active during a Full Moon. You will notice an increase in your emotional level and, quite possibly, a decrease in your logic. All Full Moons will be marked on any lunar calendar you use, often indicated by a white circle, symbolising the bright disc. There will be a least one Full Moon in every calendar month.

You can harness the Full Moon's energies by choosing this time to release and let go of things or people which are holding you back. Let yourself feel the emotions which surface – you are human, and it's OK to feel upset, afraid or anxious. Since endings and beginnings naturally follow one another – and an ending is always followed by something new – focus on the positive and look ahead towards the New Moon, when you can start to make progress.

An easy way to keep track of Full Moons and their role in your life is to use a Full Moon journal page – you can download one from the website, or make your own. Note the date, and which sign and house the Moon is in, and explore your feelings about how it is impacting your life.

Exercise: Full Moon Challenges

Think about a time in your life when you have experienced an ending – even, or especially, an ending which you did not want. Perhaps you moved home and had to change schools, or found yourself unwillingly single after the end of a relationship. Such endings are often emotional and sad, even distressing, but when the dust has settled, we invariably find that something positive and new has come along in place of what we have lost. As a result of that ending, what positive things did you experience? Can you resolve to learn from this and apply positive thinking to any endings which may come along under the influence of a Full Moon?

Full Moon Through the Signs

Each Full Moon has a slightly different energy, depending on what sign the Moon is in – and each has a slightly different focus for its energy, depending on what house the Moon is transiting at the time.

In order to best use the Full Moon's energy, first consider which sign the Moon is in. All Full Moons are ideal for moving on from difficult situations, resolving outstanding issues and finishing overdue tasks, but different emotional energies are at play. A Taurus Full Moon is a healthy time to move on from a stifling relationship, but an overly emotional Scorpio or Pisces Full Moon would make such a decision more distressing than it needs to be. A Capricorn Full Moon is perfect for finishing a difficult school project or taking an exam, but a dutiful Virgo Full Moon could make you resentful of the extra effort you have to put in. Of course, often you will have no choice on the dates when these things happen, but if you do have a choice, look carefully at the subtle differences between the Full Moon signs.

Full Moon in Aries – your self-esteem is challenged. Work on understanding how reckless or selfish behaviour might have landed you in trouble and how you can avoid it happening again.

Full Moon in Taurus – what are you obsessing about? It's time to let go of a cherished possession, stand back from a treasured project or allow a special someone space to breathe.

Full Moon in Gemini – think before you speak, because words once said cannot be undone. Complete unfinished tasks; go back to something you abandoned and do it right this time.

Full Moon in Cancer – issues from the past make a welcome or unwelcome return, stirring strong emotions. Be careful to learn from but not to become trapped in the past.

Full Moon in Leo – enjoy acclaim, success and all good things, but remember that pride really does come before a fall. Cultivate some humility.

Full Moon in Virgo – time is short, and life is busy, but are you giving up too much of yourself for others? Feelings of bitterness and resentment flourish now if you don't have enough "me" time.

Full Moon in Libra – a triumph of tact over substance. You'll say and do all of the right things at the right time, but your superficiality is being challenged and you'll long for something deeper.

Full Moon in Scorpio – what are you hiding? Secrets will out and passions run high. Expect the best but prepare for the worst in relationships and emotional bonds of all kinds.

Full Moon in Sagittarius – your open-mindedness is being challenged and you might find it hard to follow through on things you thought you believed. An unsettling time.

Full Moon in Capricorn – by keeping in with the crowd, are you hiding your true self? Your desire for status and recognition is challenged, questioned or rewarded.

Full Moon in Aquarius – are you stretching your freedom too far? Rebels without a cause will find themselves brought down a peg or two under this influence.

Full Moon in Pisces – your compassion is laudable, but you're soaking up negative as well as positive emotions from others. A tumultuous time when dreams and psychic vibes are all important.

New Moon and Full Moon Through the Houses

Of course the sign the Moon is in is only one part of the jigsaw. As you already know by now, it's very important to know which house the Moon is transiting, because its energies will be focused on that area of your life. It's sometimes difficult to understand the subtle difference between the energies of the New and Full Moons as they apply to your astrological houses, so we'll consider them both together. Remember that a New Moon's energy brings initiative and fresh starts, whereas a Full Moon's energy brings reflection, challenge and feelings. Although you can make positive changes to any aspect of your life at New Moon or Full Moon, changes will be particularly effective in the sphere of life affected by the transiting New or Full Moon.

New or Full Moon in the 1st House – reinvent yourself! This is the perfect time to change your personal image – a good excuse for new clothes or a new hairstyle! Work on your personality too, by learning how to improve your confidence and self-esteem.

New or Full Moon in the 2nd House – reinvent your finances! Set up a budget or look at ways in which you can earn some money. Think about how you can make yourself feel more secure, both emotionally and materially.

New or Full Moon in the 3rd House – expand your mind! Start new school projects, make a revision timetable, learn to communicate better. Take positive steps towards expressing yourself healthily.

New or Full Moon in the 4th House – revitalise your home! Smooth over rows at home, redecorate your room or start helping out with the chores. Work on accepting the past, even the parts of it which hurt or which you find it hard to forgive.

New or Full Moon in the 5th House – take up a new hobby! Play, sing, laugh and let your creativity shine through. Take positive steps towards making life more about fun and less about boredom.

New or Full Moon in the 6th House – increase your mojo! Harness extra willpower to shake off bad habits and make positive changes to your health. Work on timetables, filing and personal organisation.

New or Full Moon in the 7th House – feel the love! Start a new relationship or strengthen an existing one. Be honest and open about your differences and learn the gentle art of compromise.

New or Full Moon in the 8th House – get serious! Take on new responsibilities or start a spiritual quest. Explore new avenues of belief and dare to take a walk on the wild side.

New or Full Moon in the 9th House – expand your horizons! Go somewhere new, see different sights. Consciously shake off old prejudices and embrace new and unusual lifestyles.

New or Full Moon in the 10th House – soar to the stars! Take the credit you deserve, start to succeed, stop hiding your light. This is a time to be ambitious and never settle for less than you really want.

New or Full Moon in the 11th House – make new friends! Talk to someone new, share something of yourself with others. Join new social clubs and groups, talk and listen, take part in the world.

New or Full Moon in the 12th House – be kind! Resolve to live a more spiritual life, start listening to your dreams, explore your psychic potential and avoid negative secrets.

Blending the New Moon or Full Moon Sign and House Energies

Often a New or Full Moon is the catalyst for making changes in your life and you can use the Moon's sign and house position to select something you want to work on – so when you discover that the New Moon will be transiting your 11th House, you can decide to work on expanding your friendships, for example. But what if you have something specific you want to change or work on and the New or Full Moon sign and energies aren't "perfect" for it? Well, then you have to blend the sign and house energies and see how you can make them work towards your objective.

Blending sign and house energies is a tricky thing at first, and something which comes with a great deal of practice. Have a look at these examples and see if you can follow how the energies from both the sign and house are blending together.

Emily wants to use the New Moon to improve her relationship with her elder sister. The New Moon is in Leo and is transiting her 3rd House. Emily decides to build a bridge with her sister by asking for her help in planning her homework and revision time. She approaches her sister expecting an agreement, but is careful not to assume too much and tones down her words to avoid sounding arrogant.

Claire wants to use the New Moon to start a new exercise regime. The New Moon is in Aries and is transiting her 11th House. Claire is full of energy and enthusiasm for her new regime, but decides to involve her friends in a group effort so that they can all motivate each other and benefit from the social interaction. They will be there for one another so that each individual doesn't get angry with herself for not making fast enough progress.

Sophie wants to use the Full Moon to get her studies better organised. The Full Moon is in Taurus and is transiting her 12th House. Sophie makes a careful plan for her revision and considers whether she is obsessing over tiny details in order to put off the inevitable hard work. She decides to embrace a new, alternative approach, choosing meditation and visualisation to help her focus; she also resolves to be kind to herself, allowing plenty of "me" time into her schedule.

Exercise: Setting New and Full Moon Goals

Look ahead in the lunar calendar to the date of the next New Moon. Note down its sign and work out which of your houses it will be transiting. Reading the sign and house notes above, and working with your own intuition, decide what new beginning you would like to work on during the next New Moon. You can use the New Moon journal page to do this, or simply work it out in your head. Then repeat the exercise for the Full Moon following that New Moon. You will often find that what you begin during a New Moon reaches a natural high point or ending at the following Full Moon, so you might want to link your two objectives in the above exercise – for instance, set yourself a goal of working on such and such for the two weeks following New Moon, and then follow up on that after the Full Moon.

Eclipses of the Sun and Moon

Although we tend to think of eclipses as being very rare events, there are actually at least two solar eclipses every year, and there can be as many as five. There are also at least two lunar eclipses each year. Not all of these eclipses are total eclipses, so there isn't always anything very dramatic to see in the sky, but they do have an effect on our astrological energies.

A solar eclipse occurs when the Moon passes between the Sun and the Earth, and the Moon, as seen from Earth, fully or partially blocks our view of the Sun. A solar eclipse can only occur at the time of a New Moon, when the Moon and the Sun, as seen from Earth, are in conjunction. A lunar eclipse occurs when the Moon passes behind the Earth in such a manner that the Earth prevents the Sun's light from reflecting off the Moon, turning the Moon a deep red as the Earth's atmosphere scatters the sunlight. A lunar eclipse can only occur at the time of a Full Moon.

In ancient times, eclipses were frightening events for our ancestors, and were usually thought to indicate a coming disaster or crisis. The modern astrological interpretation isn't so doom-laden, but we do still find that eclipses of both the Sun and the Moon herald dramatic events, changes of fortune or turning points in our lives, whether for better or temporarily worse.

Eclipses of both the Sun and the Moon are always shown in lunar calendars, because both involve the Moon. You can easily find a list of date for forthcoming eclipses by searching online or looking on Wikipedia. Once you know the date of an eclipse, look at the lunar calendar for that date in order to work out which of your astrological houses will be affected. During a solar eclipse, the Sun and Moon are both transiting the same house, which you can work out from the Moon's position in the normal way. During a lunar eclipse, the Sun is opposite the Moon and transiting the opposite house. Because eclipses occur in pairs, with either a solar eclipse following two weeks after a lunar eclipse, or a lunar eclipse following two weeks after a solar one, we consider their astrological influence on both houses – if the solar eclipse affects your 2nd House, the lunar eclipse will affect your 8th House; if the solar eclipse is in your 5th House, the lunar eclipse will be in your 11th House and so on.

Eclipses Through the Houses

Remember that eclipses bring drama, turning points and changes of direction. Life will not be the same in the house pair areas of life following the eclipse, but much of the upheaval is eventually for good, regardless of whether or not it feels upsetting at the time. The key is to focus on the long term. It's impossible to predict exactly what effects an eclipse will have in an individual's chart, without reference to the whole natal chart, because of course all of our lives and circumstances are different. However, these are some key themes to look out for as an eclipse occurs and for the weeks and months following it. An eclipse acts as a catalyst, and a major event on or close to this date will make its repercussions known for some time afterwards.

Eclipses in the 1st and 7th Houses

The focus here is the conflict between the self and relationships. You may start a new and much wanted relationship only to struggle with a loss of identity or personal freedom. A new relationship may enhance – or detract from – your self-esteem. Your personal image and your appearance may undergo a radical shift which may lead to a new relationship – or to the ending of one which is no longer satisfactory.

Eclipses in the 2nd and 8th Houses

Here, the focus is the conflict between what you want and need, and what other people want and need from you. There is often a financial element involved, and this set of eclipses can herald a sudden influx or outflux of money, but for teens it's more likely to be a matter of security and comfort, both mental and physical. You may lose or gain a major item which provokes jealousy, or you may feel intensely resentful of someone else's changing circumstances. A gift from someone might put you under an obligation to them, or someone may try to emotionally blackmail you.

Eclipses in the 3rd and 9th Houses

In this set of eclipses, the focus is on a conflict between your skills and your dreams. Events happening now may force the issue and urge you to make a choice to pursue a dream or not, to learn something new or not, to put your talents to the test or not. You might start to teach others your skills, or to mentor someone with your outstanding communication skills. This eclipse will find you taking a new course or changing your personal philosophy due to events you witness. Your spiritual beliefs could be shaken up or you might find yourself gaining acclaim for your open mind.

Eclipses in the 4th and 10th Houses

Here, the focus is on your private life and its interplay with your status and your public life. Dramatic events within the family play out against a backdrop of worrying what the neighbours will think. Under the influence of these eclipses, your family may move home, or you may be making the move away from the family home in order to pursue your early career or higher education ambitions. Sudden changes of heart about where you want to be in life and what you want to achieve are par for the course, perhaps accompanied by dismay at home over your decisions.

Eclipses in the 5th and 11th Houses

The focus here is on friendships and group activities, and how well they do or do not match up with your own personal hobbies, creativity and joys. It can be a time of make or break in friendships and your social circle may expand or shrink dramatically at this time. Taking a risk could alienate you from a companion, or perhaps it's you who is horrified at something a friend has done. There's also tension between wanting to enjoy yourself and wanting to be more socially responsible and humanitarian. Perhaps you offer to take on some voluntary work but then find that you resent its intrusion into your own free time.

Eclipses in the 6th and 12th Houses

During this set of eclipses, the focus is on coming to terms with a situation which is not what you thought it would be. Illusions about someone or something may be shattered, daily routines are overturned and you're challenged to adapt to a whole new way of doing things. If you have deceived or been deceived, the truth will out now. It's also a time for sudden realisations about your health; perhaps you'll be spurred into making healthier life choices by having to cope with drama surrounding someone who did not.

Exercise: How Have Eclipses Affected You?

For this exercise, you'll need to look backwards in the lunar calendar. Listed below are the dates for eclipses from the first half of 2012 back to 2010. Do you recall anything happening to you on or around these dates? Look them up in a lunar calendar and work out which of your astrological houses were affected. You can use the downloadable Eclipse journal page, or just write wherever you want to.

15th January 2010 – Solar Eclipse in Capricorn
26th June 2010 – Lunar Eclipse in Capricorn
11th July 2010 – Solar Eclipse in Cancer
21st December 2010 – Lunar Eclipse in Gemini
4th January 2011 – Solar Eclipse in Capricorn
1st June 2011 – Solar Eclipse in Gemini
15th June 2011 – Lunar Eclipse in Sagittarius
1st July 2011 – Solar Eclipse in Cancer
25th November 2011 – Solar Eclipse in Sagittarius
10th December 2011 – Lunar Eclipse in Gemini
21st May 2012 – Solar Eclipse in Gemini
4th June 2012 – Lunar Eclipse in Sagittarius

Wow! You're really starting to get to grips with lunar astrology now. You've learnt about your Moon Sign and house, learnt how to follow the Moon's daily movements and about what Full Moons, New Moons and eclipses mean. Now let's look at how you can apply all this knowledge to different areas of your life.

Chapter 5

Your Moon at School

Love it or hate it, education is a major part of your life – in fact, as a teen, it's your "job". By her 18th birthday, the average British teen will have spent a whopping 17,290 hours at school – so let's see how the Moon can help to make that time more pleasant, more productive, less stressful and more meaningful.

Your lunar personality has a huge impact on the way you feel about school, and gives you a unique set of strengths and weaknesses as you study and grow. Refer back to your Lunar Personality sheet to remind yourself of how your natal Moon Sign behaves. Do you recognise yourself here? You can download a Moon at School journal sheet from the website to work through this chapter, or you can create your own.

The Aries Moon at School

You're a natural born leader at school and will always be the first to volunteer to try something new. Full of physical energy, you find it difficult to sit still for too long and probably spent most of your younger years being told off for fidgeting! Impatience with lengthy homework means that you can be slapdash in your approach – it's not that you can't do it, more that you can't be bothered to do it. Having said that, a desire to win at all costs does motivate you to try to be top of the class – when you feel like it. Emotionally, you tend to overreact to your teachers. You either love or loathe each one and are indifferent about none of them. You do work well independently, but less so in a team unless you can be in charge, so the immortal words "find a partner… " will usually leave you scowling.

Your Strongest Subjects: Science, business studies, sports

Your School Strengths: Motivation to succeed, ability to work without supervision

Your School Weaknesses: Impatience, allowing anger or bad moods to distract you

Working with Your Aries Moon at School: Try these journal prompts on your Moon at School sheet.

- How much do you agree or disagree with the description of your Aries Moon at school? Remember, the Moon is the energy of how you feel, so even if you don't behave exactly as described, is it how you'd *like* to behave?
- Think of a time when your school strengths were at their strongest. When did being self-motivated or being able to work without supervision bring you praise or a great feeling of having done well?
- Conversely, remember a time when your impatience or bad mood stopped you working at school as well as you might have done. How might you harness the strength of your Aries Moon to help you handle that differently next time?

The Taurus Moon at School

You enjoy the routines of school and you like to know what's expected of you, where to go, what to do. You have plenty of common sense and you are good at logical thought, applying yourself well to most subjects. In practical, hands-on lessons, you really come into your own, much preferring to "do" than to write or watch. With a step by step approach to study, you're not afraid to tackle big projects. Even when school is boring, you manage to maintain a sense of the bigger picture, and you understand why you're there and what it might mean for your future. However, being generally very placid by nature, you find it hard to speak up against poor teaching or anything else which needs addressing. You're also not fond of change, so upheaval caused by a new teacher, or a move to a new school or class, can throw your emotions for quite some time.

Your Strongest Subjects: Music, business studies, design

Your School Strengths: Methodical study, strong logical abilities

Your School Weaknesses: Reluctance to embrace new ideas

Working with Your Taurus Moon at School: Try these journal prompts on your Moon at School sheet.

- How much do you agree or disagree with the description of your Taurus Moon at school? Remember, the Moon is the energy of how you feel, so even if you don't behave exactly as described, is it how you'd *like* to behave?
- Think of a time when your school strengths were at their strongest. When did methodical study or a flash of logic save the day or help you get excellent results?
- Conversely, remember a time when your refusal to try something new held you back or made you miss out on a fun or rewarding opportunity. How might you harness the strength of your Taurus Moon to help you handle that differently next time?

The Gemini Moon at School

Intelligent, communicative and with a lively mind, you are a natural student and you get a lot of personal satisfaction from study and from learning new things. There is a "Jack of all trades" mentality here, though – you prefer to know a little about a lot of subjects rather than to specialise in a few. Decisions can overwhelm you when you're forced to narrow down your areas of study and you second-guess yourself all the time about whether you've made the right choices for your future. Your gregarious, sociable nature means that you get on well with most teachers and classmates, but you can be overly talkative in class. You're quite objective about criticism, not taking it personally. Time management isn't your strongest talent and you tend to leave homework and revision to the last minute, getting by on charm, wit and a healthy dose of natural ability.

Your Strongest Subjects: English, modern languages, ICT

Your School Strengths: Quick grasp of facts, enthusiasm for study

Your School Weaknesses: Ability to talk yourself into trouble, lack of focus

Working with Your Gemini Moon at School: Try these journal prompts on your Moon at School sheet.

- How much do you agree or disagree with the description of your Gemini Moon at school? Remember, the Moon is the energy of how you feel, so even if you don't behave exactly as described, is it how you'd *like* to behave?
- Think of a time when your school strengths were at their strongest. When did your enthusiasm carry you through a difficult test, or being able to quickly grasp a new concept put you ahead of the rest?
- Conversely, remember a time when trying to do too many tasks at once wasted time or stopped you finishing some important work. How might you harness the strength of your Gemini Moon to help you handle that differently next time?

The Cancer Moon at School

You have an excellent memory and you retain information effortlessly, so you have all of the tools to do well in exams and tests – but your nerves and anxieties can get the better of you when the pressure is on. You love to write and much prefer written work to having to speak up orally; you can be quiet and hesitant in class, despite having much to contribute. With lots of imaginative flair, you love art and design. Getting great marks at school is important to you, but more to please your family than for your own satisfaction. When life isn't going so well, you are easily depressed and your schoolwork can veer from excellent to poor and back again with frightening ease, depending entirely on your mood – and not only your own mood, since you're highly susceptible to the moods of classmates, teachers and friends too.

Your Strongest Subjects: Art, history, English

Your School Strengths: Strong memory, excellent writing skills

Your School Weaknesses: Uneven moods, susceptible to nerves

Working with Your Cancer Moon at School: Try these journal prompts on your Moon at School sheet.

- How much do you agree or disagree with the description of your Cancer Moon at school? Remember, the Moon is the energy of how you feel, so even if you don't behave exactly as described, is it how you'd *like* to behave?
- Think of a time when your school strengths were at their strongest. When did your excellent memory help to make homework easier? When did your ability to express yourself on paper lead to success?
- Conversely, remember a time when nerves or anxiety meant that you didn't live up to your own expectations with a piece of work or school experience. How might you harness the strength of your Cancer Moon to help you handle that differently next time?

The Leo Moon at School

Certainly not a shrinking violet at school, you like to be noticed and will seek out attention and praise. The good news is that this makes you a natural hard worker; the less great news is that it can also make you arrogant and domineering in class. You're also highly competitive and need to be top of the class in everything. With a flair for the dramatic, you feel that your school life is always either fantastic or awful, never just OK. Although you can be bossy, your creative instincts are strong and you have a lot of talent. You don't like to ask for help, however, so this can lead to you trying to cover up your weaker areas instead of addressing them head on and being able to improve. Being well organised is a big plus when it comes to complex tasks, revision or lengthy homework.

Your Strongest Subjects: Drama, design, biology, politics

Your School Strengths: Competitive nature, creative thought

Your School Weaknesses: Arrogance, failure to ask for help when needed

Working with Your Leo Moon at School: Try these journal prompts on your Moon at School sheet.

- How much do you agree or disagree with the description of your Leo Moon at school? Remember, the Moon is the energy of how you feel, so even if you don't behave exactly as described, is it how you'd *like* to behave?
- Think of a time when your school strengths were at their strongest. When did your urge to win or to be first help you do better than you would otherwise have done? When did you come up with a creative idea which won hearts and minds?
- Conversely, remember a time when arrogance or bossiness on your part meant that a team didn't do as well as you collectively should have done, or when you struggled on with a difficult piece of work instead of just asking for help? How might you harness the strength of your Leo Moon to help you handle that differently next time?

The Virgo Moon at School

Intelligent, diligent and hard-working, your teachers probably consider you a model student. You always get your homework done on time, and maintain neat books and folders. A lack of self-confidence does mean that you're one of the quieter people in class, however, and you don't always speak up when you need help – or, for that matter, to share your brilliance with everyone else. If you're facing a teacher you don't like, or if you have problems with bullying, your health can flare up quite badly, so for you school nerves, stomach aches and headaches can be very real indeed. You don't always realise how much talent you have, being your own worst critic, so it's helpful to you when others praise your work – all you have to do then is find it in yourself to believe the glowing reports and to promote your own talents instead of waiting for the world to beat a path to your door!

Your Strongest Subjects: English, science, economics

Your School Strengths: Hard work, attention to detail

Your School Weaknesses: Reticence, lack of self-belief

Working with Your Virgo Moon at School: Try these journal prompts on your Moon at School sheet.

- How much do you agree or disagree with the description of your Virgo Moon at school? Remember, the Moon is the energy of how you feel, so even if you don't behave exactly as described, is it how you'd *like* to behave?
- Think of a time when your school strengths were at their strongest. When did your attention to detail help you keep an important piece of work on track? When did sheer hard work pay off in exam results or recognition?
- Conversely, remember a time when you missed out on credit you were due because you didn't speak up to claim an idea or let someone else take over your limelight. Was there a time when you regret not speaking up in class? How might you harness the strength of your Virgo Moon to help you handle that differently next time?

The Libra Moon at School

Sociable and often highly popular, you breeze through school on your wits and charm. You're very bright, but you don't always choose to work as hard as you might, preferring to get by on a minimum amount of effort. Having said that, you do have enormous talent in music and the arts and these will always command your full attention. Equality and fairness at school are very important to you and you will enjoy sitting on a school council or making your voice heard on the current issues of the day. Your natural kindness and empathy make you a natural student mentor or guide. Because you are so keen to be liked, however, you do sometimes find yourself mixing with the wrong crowd, and doing things you would not normally do in order to find favour. Easily led, you are sometimes the scapegoat for more wily friends' escapades.

Your Strongest Subjects: Art, music, design

Your School Strengths: Social skills, diplomacy

Your School Weaknesses: Coasting, easily influenced by others

Working with Your Libra Moon at School: Try these journal prompts on your Moon at School sheet.

- How much do you agree or disagree with the description of your Libra Moon at school? Remember, the Moon is the energy of how you feel, so even if you don't behave exactly as described, is it how you'd *like* to behave?
- Think of a time when your school strengths were at their strongest. When did your social skills help you attract support for a pet project or round up the perfect team for a particular task? When were you able to defuse tension in a group by using your diplomatic skills?
- Conversely, remember a time when you know you simply did not put in as much effort as you should have done. Do you regret that now? How about a time when you've gone along with the group and wish you'd spoken out differently instead? How might you harness the strength of your Libra Moon to help you handle that differently next time?

The Scorpio Moon at School

You are a resourceful and passionate student, and you are

enormously determined in the subjects which interest you most. You have strong feelings about everything and are incapable of just "not minding", whether it's a teacher, a subject or the décor of your classroom. With a strong memory, you tend to do well in exams, but your approach to revision is a bit on the obsessive side. Of all the signs, you are the most likely to be bored by dumbed down lessons, as you either don't care for the subject at all or you want to explore it intensely and in depth. Self-discipline is not a problem, but your unpredictable moods can sometimes leave you feeling isolated among your peers. You do hold grudges and will not forgive a teacher or classmate who lets you down, betrays your trust or otherwise falls short of the high standards you expect.

Your Strongest Subjects: Maths, science, law

Your School Strengths: Resourcefulness, research skills

Your School Weaknesses: Taking criticism personally, boredom

Working with Your Scorpio Moon at School: Try these journal prompts on your Moon at School sheet.

- How much do you agree or disagree with the description of your Scorpio Moon at school? Remember, the Moon is the energy of how you feel, so even if you don't behave exactly as described, is it how you'd *like* to behave?
- Think of a time when your school strengths were at their strongest. When have you managed to find just the right website or just the right person to help you with a difficult problem? When were you the one who came up with an ingenious solution which won praise and admiration?
- Conversely, remember a time when you know your personal attitude towards a teacher or classmate stood in the way of your education. Think also about a time when you switched off completely from boring lessons or let poor teaching turn you off a subject you might otherwise have enjoyed. How might you harness the strength of your

Scorpio Moon to help you handle that differently next time?

The Sagittarius Moon at School

Positive, optimistic, outgoing, sporty and bright, you seem to have everything going for you at school, with plenty of friends and a healthy interest in subjects across the curriculum. You're extremely independent, however, and you struggle more than people realise with the concept of someone else telling you what you should know and what you must learn. You like to think out loud and to argue a case from several different standpoints at once, and you are a very persuasive leader in school tasks. Your rebellious streak may land you in trouble, but in truth you're rather glad that it does. You challenge rules wherever you find them and you will do everything in your power to organise your own education, your way… so relationships with teachers can be fraught at times, and with parents too if they find it hard to understand your attitude.

Your Strongest Subjects: Philosophy, business studies, geography

Your School Strengths: Questioning nature, independence

Your School Weaknesses: Rebellion (although this can be a plus), lack of respect for authority

Working with Your Sagittarius Moon at School: Try these journal prompts on your Moon at School sheet.

- How much do you agree or disagree with the description of your Sagittarius Moon at school? Remember, the Moon is the energy of how you feel, so even if you don't behave exactly as described, is it how you'd *like* to behave?
- Think of a time when your school strengths were at their strongest. When have you questioned what you are being taught and successfully learnt something from the ensuing debate? Does being able to work alone have any advan-

tages for you?

- Conversely, remember a time when you know that you've been rebellious for no particular reason. How much time did it waste, and would you do it differently if you could go back in time? Is there a time when you showed disrespect towards a teacher and you now wish that you hadn't? How might you harness the strength of your Sagittarius Moon to help you handle that differently next time?

The Capricorn Moon at School

Ambitious but private, determined but patient, you have the tools to excel at school. You're very well organised and practical and you love the more hands-on subjects. You apply yourself well and will work steadily towards a goal even when you don't particularly enjoy a subject. Responsible and mature, you work well when given a specific role at school – prefect, mentor or the like is definitely something you would love. Since you tend to keep yourself to yourself, however, you sometimes struggle to widen your social circle at school. You are very keen to "prove" yourself and will hate to have to ask for or accept help from anyone, even a friend, and you're very hard on yourself if you feel that you're failing in any way – in this way, you can be your own worst enemy.

Your Strongest Subjects: Maths, economics, IT

Your School Strengths: Ambition, responsible nature

Your School Weaknesses: Unwillingness to accept help, isolation

Working with Your Capricorn Moon at School: Try these journal prompts on your Moon at School sheet.

- How much do you agree or disagree with the description of your Capricorn Moon at school? Remember, the Moon is the energy of how you feel, so even if you don't behave exactly as described, is it how you'd *like* to behave?

- Think of a time when your school strengths were at their strongest. Does your innate ambition motivate you to always do your best? Think of a time when taking on extra responsibility helped you feel good about yourself.
- Conversely, remember a time when you struggled on, not really understanding a topic, but not wanting to ask for help either. Are there times when your lack of confidence has held you back from spreading your social wings at school? How might you harness the strength of your Capricorn Moon to help you handle that differently next time?

The Aquarius Moon at School

A round peg in a square hole, you feel slightly different at school. You have an intuitive grasp of how one subject links with another and how the humanities blend with the arts, which blend with the sciences and so on. You're friendly and gregarious, but you form many "light" friendships rather than a handful of deeper ones. Ever the humanitarian, you're far more concerned with saving the planet than you are with learning how to make money, and you'll often find yourself questioning the point of school, and indeed of "the establishment" as a whole. A deep thinker, others consider you either slightly odd or ahead of your time, and teachers can become exasperated when your clever mind refuses to stay in the box they've created for it. Unpredictability can also land you in trouble, because you sometimes just don't realise – or care – what impact your actions will have.

Your Strongest Subjects: Technology, geography, environmental science

Your School Strengths: Unorthodox insights, "big picture" understanding

Your School Weaknesses: Unpredictability, detachment

Working with Your Aquarius Moon at School: Try these journal prompts on your Moon at School sheet.

- How much do you agree or disagree with the description of your Aquarius Moon at school? Remember, the Moon is the energy of how you feel, so even if you don't behave exactly as described, is it how you'd *like* to behave?
- Think of a time when your school strengths were at their strongest. When did you think laterally and manage to help others do likewise? When did your wider perspective help you to make cross-curricular links and show a wider understanding than your peers?
- Conversely, remember a time when you disobeyed a rule, turned up late, didn't turn up at all or otherwise did something unpredictable which had negative results for you. Are there times when you feel as though you're just going through the motions at school? How might you harness the strength of your Aquarius Moon to help you handle that differently next time?

The Pisces Moon at School

Highly emotional and sensitive, school can be a place of real drama for you, at both the wonderful and the awful ends of the scale. You are easily wounded by even the most positive of criticism, and you are easily distracted by even the most boring of distractions. Focus and concentration can be tough for you, but when you do manage to pay attention, you can produce outstandingly creative work, with an enormous flair for art, crafts and language. The most likely of all signs to be negatively affected by peer pressure, you do find it difficult to stand up to or against others, and need a strong support network of close friends and family in order to really thrive at school. You have (very) favourite teachers and subjects which drive you to tears, but above all you live and sense every single moment of your school career with a depth no other sign can match.

Your Strongest Subjects: Languages, English, art

Your School Strengths: Creativity, compassion

Your School Weaknesses: Susceptibility to peer pressure, oversensitivity

Working with Your Pisces Moon at School: Try these journal prompts on your Moon at School sheet.

- How much do you agree or disagree with the description of your Pisces Moon at school? Remember, the Moon is the energy of how you feel, so even if you don't behave exactly as described, is it how you'd *like* to behave?
- Think of a time when your school strengths were at their strongest. When did your imagination and creativity win praise from others? Have you made a difference to someone's school life through your compassion?
- Conversely, remember a time when you gave in to peer pressure and regretted it, or when you allowed a negative mark or comment to plunge you into the depths of despair. How might you harness the strength of your Pisces Moon to help you handle that differently next time?

Your 12 School Moods

OK, so now you know how your Moon Sign, your lunar personality, affects your general attitude towards school. Consider it an overall flavour of how you are as a student. As the Moon progresses through the 12 houses each month, your mood at school will subtly change. You will always remain true to your Moon Sign – so an unconventional Aquarius Moon personality isn't suddenly going to turn into a cautious, common sense-filled Taurus Moon personality, but within the background flavour that your Moon Sign provides, your focus will shift.

School Moon Transiting 1st House

Open and honest with a healthy touch of sassy, you're genuinely interested in school during this transit, but you also want to make an impression. Whether it's tampering with the uniform or breaking the make-up rules, how you look at school will have a subtle influence on how you feel right now.

School Moon Transiting 2nd House

Time to play it safe. During this transit, you'll stick to the rules and not want to rock the boat. Habits are easy to form and hard to break under a 2nd House Moon. Anything which takes you out of your comfort zone will not be welcomed.

School Moon Transiting 3rd House

This is the natural student transit. Learning becomes much easier for a few days and everything educational falls into place. Your communication skills will increase, both orally and in writing, but you might struggle with keeping quiet in class.

School Moon Transiting 4th House

A lazy, somewhat lethargic transit – duvet day, anyone? You wish! Focus and concentration don't come all that easily for a couple of days, but you'll nevertheless do your best at school (once you finally get there!) because you do want to please parents and other authority figures.

School Moon Transiting 5th House

It's all about the fun! Lots of energy at school during this transit, so it's perfect for sports, drama and anything creative. Ordinary desk work… not so ideal. You're pretty restless, but it's a good time to join a new school club or make new friends.

School Moon Transiting 6th House

Time to knuckle down. Sheer hard work is what this transit is all about and it's perfect for getting stuck in to coursework, big projects and anything you normally try to avoid. Very organised too, so ideal for planning a revision timetable or clearing your desk.

School Moon Transiting 7th House

AKA the love transit. What can I say? Your mind's not on your schoolwork. Whether you're single or loved up, for a few days it's all about him (or potential hims), flirting and being ever so, ever so concerned about what other people think of you. Potentially difficult if this transit coincides with a heavy workload.

School Moon Transiting 8th House

Boredom is quick to set in under this transit unless you have outstanding teachers. Use the time to do some of your own research, read around your subject and take your knowledge further than the curriculum allows. Try hard not to get distracted by juicy gossip!

School Moon Transiting 9th House

This is a taking stock transit. Look at how you're doing so far at school this month, this term, this year. You're very objective now and you can clearly see where you need to improve. Set yourself some goals and get stuck in.

School Moon Transiting 10th House

Power, status and ambition – what you're interested in now is not what's going on at school, but where it's all heading and what you can expect to get as a reward for all this hard work in the future. Very career focused, this is superb time for looking ahead to higher education or work.

School Moon Transiting 11th House

Academics are not high up your priority list under this transit. Instead, you're focusing on the social aspects of school. Friendships could be made or broken, tested or repaired, all against the heady backdrop of double maths. Definitely an interesting few days.

School Moon Transiting 12th House

Fabulously imaginative and creative, this transit is also known for its deceptive qualities. If the need arises for the dog to have eaten your homework, you won't hesitate to say so. Little white lies apart, however, it's a wonderful few days for developing your artistic and literary talents at school.

Exercise: Tracking Your School Moods

Find out which house your moon is transiting today. How does that match up with what you've experienced at school today? Remember to blend in the overall energies of your Moon Sign too. If you can track this every day for one whole moon cycle – 28 days – then at the end of that cycle you'll start to notice patterns repeating. Use the downloadable Moon at School journal page to keep track, or just make notes in your journal as you go along.

Examples:

Cancer Moon Personality when the School Moon is transiting the 11th House – you'll pick up on friends' moods even more easily, which can be unsettling and can lead to trouble in class. Your family may be dismayed at how much time you're spending socialising instead of working.

Libra Moon Personality when the School Moon is transiting the 12th House – it's all too easy to ignore homework and school demands, and you might also be caught up in covering for friends or wriggling your way out of trouble with something only vaguely resembling the truth.

Capricorn Moon Personality when the School Moon is transiting the 3rd House – you won't need to put in quite so much work in order to get good results, and you'll feel more confident about speaking out, asking for help and getting involved.

Using the Moon to Help with School Issues and Decisions

As well as tracking the Moon's movements through your chart

and understanding how this can affect your moods and attitude at school, you can also be more proactive with using the Moon's energies. For most common situations, there are some lunar energies, signs and houses which are more helpful than others, and if you have the chance to plan ahead it helps to know which days might be best for handling certain things. Of course you won't always have a choice, but when you do, try to choose the following moon transits and energies when you:

Start a major piece of work/coursework – moon in Aries (for initiative) or Capricorn (for staying power), moon transiting your 6th or 10th House.

Plan a revision timetable – moon in sensible Taurus or organised Virgo, moon transiting your 4th or 6th House.

Ask a teacher for help – moon in Libra (for charm) or Scorpio (for depth of knowledge), moon transiting your 3rd or 10th House.

Ask a teach for more demanding work – moon in noble Leo or expansive Sagittarius, moon transiting your 8th House

Visit a careers fair/office – moon in Leo or Capricorn, two of the most ambitious signs, moon transiting your 3rd or 10th House.

Join a new club or group – moon in sociable Gemini or charming Libra, moon transiting your 5th or 11th House.

Read around your subject – moon in penetrating Scorpio or dutiful Cancer, moon transiting your 8th or 9th House.

Focus on the arts – moon in Cancer, Libra or Pisces, all highly artistic signs, moon transiting your 1st, 5th or 12th House.

Focus on maths or science – moon in Aquarius, Scorpio or Capricorn, all signs which excel in maths and science, moon transiting your 8th House.

Focus on English or foreign languages – moon in any of the most loquacious signs Gemini, Cancer, Virgo or Pisces, moon transiting your 3rd or 9th House.

Focus on humanities and social sciences – moon in Cancer,

Sagittarius, Scorpio or Aquarius, all humanitarian or nurturing signs, moon transiting your 3rd, 6th, 8th or 9th House.

Focus on business and economics – moon in any of the most business-like signs – Aries, Taurus, Leo, Virgo, Sagittarius or Capricorn, moon transiting your 2nd or 10th House.

Start a new school – moon in Gemini (for sociability), Leo (for courage) or Libra (for charm), moon transiting your 1st, 5th, 7th or 11th House.

Discuss school with your parents – moon in Cancer (for family strength), Pisces (for understanding) or Virgo (for stability), moon transiting your 3rd or 4th House.

Report a bully – moon in courageous Aries or fair-minded Aquarius, moon transiting your 9th or 11th House.

Catch up on overdue work – moon in Virgo or Capricorn for staying power and willpower, moon transiting your 6th House.

Take a written test or exam – moon in Cancer or Scorpio, both signs noted for their memory, moon transiting your 3rd House.

Take a practical test or exam – moon in Aries (for sheer panache), Taurus or Capricorn (both for practical abilities), moon transiting your 4th or 6th House.

Don't panic if the "right" Moon Sign or house transit doesn't fit with what you need or want to do! Any tasks, at any time, will be easier to manage if you refer back to what you already know about your lunar personality and its strengths and weaknesses, both in school and in everyday life. If you have to do something awkward or difficult on a day when the Moon Sign or house transit isn't ideal, find out which sign the Moon will be in on that day, and which of your houses it will be transiting. Think carefully about the energies in play – what can you do to make the most of the Moon's energies, and to minimise any particular problems?

Chapter 6

Your Moon at Home

Families, eh? They're our strongest support system, yet at times the source of huge tension, pressure and expectation. If things are not going well at home, it's hard to give any other of life your full attention. Home should be a place of sanctuary and relaxation and when your family life is harmonious, home is your perfect space. When it's not going so well, home can be a place of anxiety, or somewhere to avoid rather than to gladly retreat. Fortunately, for most of us, the good in our family lives far outweighs the less than perfect. Using the Moon's energies, you can make your family relationships even more healthy and happy, and learn how to bring peace and resolution when discord does strike.

Your lunar personality forms the basis of how you feel about your family and how you behave at home. Refer back to your lunar personality sheet to remind yourself of your Moon Sign qualities. Let's take a look at this in more detail. You can use the Your Moon at Home journal sheet (downloadable from the website) or you can create your own journal pages, as you prefer.

The Aries Moon at Home

The family dynamo! You're restless and energetic, so home isn't a dull place when you're around. You do have a relatively short fuse, however, so the excitement isn't always of the pleasant variety. For someone with such an assertive nature, you're also surprisingly easily hurt, especially by family members, and you can take careless words to heart much more than people realise. You can't stand clutter, so you like your bedroom simple and modern. You'll pitch in with the household chores willingly enough, provided you can see that everyone else is doing their fair share too. When it comes to supporting other family members, you're a true champion and will always encourage, stand by and cheerlead for your parents and brothers and sisters. In public, that is. Privately, you want to be the most successful sibling and your competitive nature does struggle with giving others their turn in the limelight. Highly independent, you are not a natural rule follower, so if your parents are strict there will be tensions. You make decisions quickly too, so when there is a family crisis or a choice to be made, you don't like to have to wait to find out what has been decided.

As a sister, you are: Fun, competitive, inspirational

Reacting to parental authority, you are: Challenging, independent

Your family strengths: Loyalty, sense of adventure

Your family weakness: Impatience

Working with Your Aries Moon at Home: Try these journal prompts on your Moon at Home sheet.

- How much do you agree or disagree with the description of your Aries Moon at home? Remember, the Moon is the energy of how you feel, so even if you don't behave exactly as described, is it how you'd *like* to behave?
- Think of a time when you have inspired a brother or sister, or when your sense of fun has rescued the family from the doldrums. When did your loyalty help to bring the family closer or to support a loved one in a crisis?
- Conversely, remember a time when your impatience has made a row worse or has complicated a family decision. What about the last time you defied your parents' authority? How did that work out, and how might you harness the strengths of your Aries Moon to deal with it better next time?

The Taurus Moon at Home

Your family and your home are tremendously important to your sense of emotional security, and you will feel the effects even more than most when things are not well at home. Defensive and possessive of your parents and siblings, you can be jealous of siblings' friends or of a new partner for a parent. You are very practical by nature, however, and will be a huge help in finding sensible solutions to issues, showing patience and maturity when it comes to family decisions. Your tastefully decorated bedroom is an extension of you and is a warm and comfortable haven – the borders of which you will defend at all costs against sibling intrusion… Taurus doesn't "do" sharing. Taurus doesn't really "do" chores either, being slightly too selfish to muck in willingly. Except for cooking – you like cooking. Sibling rivalry isn't often a problem for you, because you accept and honour both your own talents and nature, and those of your brothers and sisters. You can be exceptionally stubborn, however, and won't appreciate a sibling who thinks they know better. You accept rules at home because you like to know where you stand. Your cautious nature doesn't often feel the need to break those rules, so arguments over personal freedom rarely arise.

As a sister, you are: Reliable, honest, practical

Reacting to parental authority, you are: Mature, sensible

Your family strengths: Common sense, emotional stability

Your family weakness: Selfishness

Working with Your Taurus Moon at Home: Try these journal prompts on your Moon at Home sheet.

- How much do you agree or disagree with the description of your Taurus Moon at home? Remember, the Moon is the energy of how you feel, so even if you don't behave exactly as described, is it how you'd *like* to behave?
- Think of a time when you have been able to offer practical help to a brother or sister, or when your common sense has

intervened in a family dispute. Does your emotional stability provide a rock for other more flighty members of the family?

- Conversely, remember a time when your selfishness has caused a row or when you know that you really should have given way in an argument. Does your tolerance of family rules ever hold you back? How might you use the strengths of your Taurus Moon to safely spread your wings a little further?

The Gemini Moon at Home

Talkative, chatty and witty, you're a fun member of the family and one who isn't overly emotional. You're more than capable of looking at your family relationships logically, and any arguments tend to blow over quite quickly from your end. You do get bored easily and will push for an active, sporty or energetic family life, always wanting to be out and about doing something or going somewhere, which can be exhausting for parents or siblings who are more homebodies at heart. You'll deal with household chores cheerfully enough but you tend to leave things half done – your bedroom is in a perpetual state of chaos, filled with books and gadgets. You form a close and loving bond with siblings, but are not above using your superior intellect and communication skills to out-talk them in an argument. Sibling rivalry is low key because you exist happily within your own little world and have enough self-belief to allow brothers and sisters to shine too. When it comes to family rules, however, you are apt to conveniently "forget" what you promised. You rely on charm and debating skills to win you extra freedom as you grow up, but you do worry your parents by not sticking to agreed arrangements.

As a sister, you are: Chatty, appreciative, charming
Reacting to parental authority, you are: Argumentative, careless
Your family strengths: Cheerfulness, communication

Your family weakness: Boredom

Working with Your Gemini Moon at Home: Try these journal prompts on your Moon at Home sheet.

- How much do you agree or disagree with the description of your Gemini Moon at home? Remember, the Moon is the energy of how you feel, so even if you don't behave exactly as described, is it how you'd *like* to behave?
- Think of a time when you have considered a sibling more of a best friend than a sibling. Does your logical mind and cool emotion help you when arguments erupt? When did your ability to talk things through help avert a family crisis?
- Conversely, remember a time when your boredom with family routines has hurt (or simply worn out!) a loved one. How about the last time you didn't stick to an agreement with your parents? How did that turn out, and how might you harness the strengths of your Gemini Moon to try things differently next time?

The Cancer Moon at Home

Home is truly where your heart is, and you are extremely close to and emotionally dependent on your family. Deeply emotional but at times moody, you want parents and siblings to understand your feelings at all times, and, to be fair, you do strive to understand theirs too. A natural homemaker, your bedroom is cosy and filled with nick-nacks and memories. You find it easy to help organise the home and you happily take on some of the household chores, taking pride in helping to maintain a welcoming home. Being so close to your family provides you with great inner strength, but it can also mean that you are sometimes fearful of growing up, moving away, or upsetting or letting down your parents, whether in a real or imagined way. You are a compassionate and nurturing sister, always there for a sibling who needs you, and you go out of your way to create mutually supportive bonds. Your tendency to offer unsolicited advice or to "baby" brothers and sisters (even older ones!) can feel suffocating to some, though, and care is needed to ensure that you neither end up making a sibling feel trapped nor take on too many of their worries and anxieties yourself.

As a sister, you are: (Over?) Protective, compassionate, wise

Reacting to parental authority, you are: Dutiful, understanding

Your family strengths: Nurturing, supportive

Your family weakness: Over-dependence

Working with Your Cancer Moon at Home: Try these journal prompts on your Moon at Home sheet.

- How much do you agree or disagree with the description of your Cancer Moon at home? Remember, the Moon is the energy of how you feel, so even if you don't behave exactly as described, is it how you'd *like* to behave?
- Think of a time when you have been rightly concerned for a parent, brother or sister and have been able to offer some wise advice. When has your compassion and support made a true difference to a loved one, and how did that make you feel?
- Conversely, remember a time when your offers of help and advice have been seen as unwanted interference. Were you hurt? Think too of a time when your reluctance to upset a family member meant turning down an opportunity or not doing something you would really have liked to do. How might you harness the strengths of your Cancer Moon to deal with these situations in the future?

The Leo Moon at Home

Here comes the drama queen! Your moods vary wildly from optimistic and lovable to dictatorial and mean, but you always add major intensity to any family situation, for better and for worse. When it comes to making family decisions, you believe that your voice should be given greater weight than it is, and your sulks if the decision doesn't go your way are legendary. Most of the time, however, your sunny nature makes the home a warm and loving place to be, and you are a very generous sibling when you're not bossing brothers and sisters about or plotting to steal the limelight. As befits regal Leo, you view chores as something servants (especially mums) do, and you take advantage of being waited on hand and foot. Your room is likely to be elegant and immaculate... but not tidied by you! Fortunately for you, your charm and general joie de vivre mean that others don't really mind your more arrogant traits. You don't always dish out the respect that you expect to receive from others, however, so parents may bemoan that you pay little attention to their wisdom. Certainly when it comes to personal freedom, you are a little overconfident in your abilities, and feel older than you are – which can lead to some difficult situations with rule breaking.

As a sister, you are: Controlling, creative, generous

Reacting to parental authority, you are: Overconfident, disrespectful

Your family strengths: Warmth, intensity, passion

Your family weakness: Arrogance

Working with Your Leo Moon at Home: Try these journal prompts on your Moon at Home sheet.

- How much do you agree or disagree with the description of your Leo Moon at home? Remember, the Moon is the energy of how you feel, so even if you don't behave exactly as described, is it how you'd *like* to behave?
- Think of a time when you have been generous with a sibling, not only with possessions, but with your time, love or advice. When has your creative instinct or your sheer strength of passion helped a family member or inspired the

family as a whole? What about a time when you were upset but managed to bounce back quickly due to your sunny nature?

- Conversely, remember a time when your disregard for a parent's authority has caused problems at home. Was there a time when your overconfidence led you into trouble? How about the last time you created a drama – did that impact negatively on a brother or sister? How might you use the strengths of your Leo Moon to deal with these issues differently next time?

The Virgo Moon at Home

A serious-minded family member, you are a rock of stability in the home. What others might not realise is that you're extremely easily hurt – you don't show your hurt with big tantrums or a fuss, but emotionally you are very sensitive within the family. You love your siblings very much, but you have a clear view of their failings as well as their strengths… and you don't hesitate to tell them so. Criticism can make brothers and sisters feel second best, but in turn you are easily made to feel second best by a sibling with a more forceful Moon, Sun or Ascendant, so sibling rivalry is a delicate and ever-changing balance. Responsible and meticulous, you like to help keep the home organised and running well, but your bedroom isn't necessarily tidy. Organised chaos is very Virgo. You don't always speak your mind at home, even in an argument, so it's sometimes difficult for family members to understand how to please or help you. You are a very supportive daughter or sister, however, and will work hard behind the scenes to help others succeed, never expecting or requiring the same in return. You won't overtly challenge parental authority, but you do have a knack of subtly subverting rules you don't agree with, often without anyone realising!

As a sister, you are: Unassuming, helpful, critical

Reacting to parental authority, you are: Quietly rebellious, respectful

Your family strengths: Responsibility, adaptability

Your family weakness: Reticence

Working with Your Virgo Moon at Home: Try these journal prompts on your Moon at Home sheet.

- How much do you agree or disagree with the description of your Virgo Moon at home? Remember, the Moon is the energy of how you feel, so even if you don't behave exactly as described, is it how you'd *like* to behave?
- Think of a time when you have put your own interests aside in order to help a brother or sister. Were you proud to be their rock? When did your responsible nature mean that you were able to take charge of part of a family project or problem?
- Conversely, remember a time when your reticence to share your emotions meant that others hurt you without meaning to. How did you think they would or should know how you felt? Remember a time when your criticism of a parent or sibling was seen as harsh rather than helpful. How about the last time you didn't agree with or stick to a parent's decision. What did you do, and how can you use the strengths of your Virgo Moon to handle the situation next time?

The Libra Moon at Home

Harmony is absolutely essential to your emotional well-being and any discord at home weighs heavily on other aspects of your daily life. As a family member, you are calm, tolerant and loving, and an excellent diplomat. You will make it your mission to smooth over arguments and problems, but you do tend to settle for superficial "niceness", which sometimes leaves deeper problems unresolved. You are appreciative of the good things in your home, but reluctant to expend any energy on keeping the household running. Your room reflects your stylish tastes, with your wardrobe busting at the seams. As a sister, you are easy-going and good-humoured, so siblings have to work hard to provoke you. Your need to please, and to be loved, can lead to you being easily manipulated by siblings, or becoming overly dependent on their approval. Relationships with your parents are warm, sincere and respectful and you are usually happy to toe the line on rules and decisions your parents impose or make, trusting that your voice has been heard and considered even if you don't get your own way. One thing you won't stand for, however, is unfairness. Any hint that a sibling is being treated differently to you will cause petulance and sulkiness, with your trademark cry of 'It's not fair!'

As a sister, you are: Tolerant, easily manipulated, easy-going

Reacting to parental authority, you are: Relaxed, trusting

Your family strengths: Diplomacy, good humour

Your family weakness: Superficiality

Working with Your Libra Moon at Home: Try these journal prompts on your Moon at Home sheet.

- How much do you agree or disagree with the description of your Libra Moon at home? Remember, the Moon is the energy of how you feel, so even if you don't behave exactly as described, is it how you'd *like* to behave?
- Think of a time when your tolerance has made a difference to the life of a brother or sister. What were you happy to put up with which made their lives better? What about a time when your diplomacy skills were able to bring together warring family members and cut short an argument before it took root? Can you think of a time when your relaxed acceptance of a family ruling saved you the hassle, anxiety or problems that someone else might have encountered?

- Conversely, remember a time when a brother or sister has manipulated you or taken advantage of your good nature. What about a time when you were happy to settle for superficial peace and ignored the deeper problems in a family conflict? Did that go on to cause problems later when these issues resurfaced? How might you harness the strengths of your Libra Moon to deal with that differently next time?

The Scorpio Moon at Home

Deep, intense and quite secretive, it's not always easy for family members to figure you out. You have an exceptional intuition and piercing insight which gets to the heart of family problems when they occur – perhaps to the discomfort of some. Although you love your family deeply, privacy is important to you and you do need, emotionally, to spend a good deal of time alone in your room. Reflecting your sensual and exotic tastes, your bedroom isn't your average teen girl's bedroom, and is probably something of a no-go zone for the rest of the family. You are courageously protective of brothers and sisters, but also quite manipulative – and yes, there is a hint of a spiteful streak in there too, which perhaps doesn't allow family rows to die down as quickly as they otherwise would. Jealousy and intense sibling rivalry becomes more of an issue the older you get, and centres especially around boyfriends and girlfriends of your siblings rather than on their achievements or on the attention they get from your parents. You don't take kindly to having rules imposed on you, however much you respect your parents, and you always think you know better, so personal freedom issues are an intense battleground.

As a sister, you are: Private, protective, manipulative

Reacting to parental authority, you are: Passionate, confrontational

Your family strengths: Intuition, perception

Your family weakness: Jealousy

Working with Your Scorpio Moon at Home: Try these journal prompts on your Moon at Home sheet.

- How much do you agree or disagree with the description of your Scorpio Moon at home? Remember, the Moon is the energy of how you feel, so even if you don't behave exactly as described, is it how you'd *like* to behave?
- Think of a time when you have been able to quickly get to the root of a family problem, saving time and drama in the process. How does your high level of perception help your family relationships? What about your need for privacy? How does this impact on other family members?
- Conversely, remember a time when your jealousy has caused problems for the family. How about the last time you confronted your parents over something you disagreed with? Or a time when you know you manipulated a brother or sister for your own ends. How did that make you feel? How might you use the strengths of your Scorpio Moon to handle things another way next time?

The Sagittarius Moon at Home

As with every other sphere of your life, freedom is a key word in your home life. You don't exactly thrive under too many rules and you long to spread your wings. Generally cheery and optimistic by nature, your sometimes sharp temper is softened with humour, and family rows involving you don't linger on. You're a natural leader and will definitely be a sister to look up to, but your off-hand comments and "see if I care" front can be hurtful at times. Family decisions never happen quickly enough for your liking, because you don't see the point in going over details or taking too long to make up your mind. Restrictions on how late you can stay out, where you can go, what you can do or who you can see are suffocating, which can cause issues if your parents have certain expectations. You do respect their authority, however, provided they play by the rules too – one thing you won't stand for is double standards. Your inherent idealism means that you sometimes imagine that everyone else's family is perfect, which leads you to question your own. When it comes to your room, you like lots of space so you won't clutter it up – but chores, to your mind, are a complete waste of time!

As a sister, you are: A role model, idealistic, fair

Reacting to parental authority, you are: Obstinate, rational

Your family strengths: Optimism, honesty

Your family weakness: Tactlessness

Working with Your Sagittarius Moon at Home: Try these journal prompts on your Moon at Home sheet.

- How much do you agree or disagree with the description of your Sagittarius Moon at home? Remember, the Moon is the energy of how you feel, so even if you don't behave exactly as described, is it how you'd *like* to behave?
- Think of a time when you have been able to act as a positive role model for a sibling, or when your sense of fairness has enabled you to accept a quarrel resolution without pushing for too much. Have your idealistic views positively influenced a family member?
- Conversely, remember a time when your tactlessness has hurt someone. How did you react to that? Think of a time when your personal freedom at home was under threat and you reacted by pushing the point or carelessly hurting a family member in your anger. How might you use the strengths of your Sagittarius Moon to handle these situations better next time?

The Capricorn Moon at Home

Cool and calm on the surface, you don't give away many emotions, even to your close family members. It takes a lot for you to reveal how you truly feel, but when you feel safe and loved your home is one place where you can be yourself. Somewhat sentimental and surprisingly soft-hearted, you love to act as a guide or teacher for younger siblings, and may be slightly in awe of older ones. Sibling rivalry isn't usually a problem but you do take yourself very seriously and can get very upset with a brother or sister's teasing. You are a thoughtful voice in family discussions and decisions, and your parents find you very trustworthy and reliable. Patience is a strong point and you don't mind how long it takes to do what must be done. You will respectfully abide by any family rules, even if you don't agree with them – but that's not to say you won't enjoy a walk on the wild side as your freedom increases. In fact, because you prove yourself to be very mature, you're likely to enjoy more leeway than others might. A tidy, well-organised bedroom is filled with study books and techno gadgets, and your helpfulness around the house is an extension of your practical, get-on-with-it nature.

As a sister, you are: Responsible, respectful, sentimental

Reacting to parental authority, you are: Calm, trustworthy

Your family strengths: Maturity, patience

Your family weakness: Emotional aloofness

Working with Your Capricorn Moon at Home: Try these journal prompts on your Moon at Home sheet.

- How much do you agree or disagree with the description of your Capricorn Moon at home? Remember, the Moon is the energy of how you feel, so even if you don't behave exactly as described, is it how you'd *like* to behave?
- Think of a time when you have been shown great trust by your parents. Were you able to live up to their expectations? When have you taught, guided or led a sibling, to great effect? When has your patience helped to defuse a difficult family situation?
- Conversely, remember a time when your reluctance to

show emotions has left your family feeling cut off from you. Has there been a time when you've been too serious for your own good and either missed out on or stopped family fun? How might you harness the strengths of your Capricorn Moon to be more confident in handling your emotions and letting go?

The Aquarius Moon at Home

The quintessential teen rebel, you are at once a fascinating but challenging member of your family, always questioning authority, always coming up with "out there" ideas you want the family to take up, particularly relating to big world issues, environmental concerns or humanitarian causes. You show an at times cynical or even contemptuous disregard for big occasions or family traditions, and don't understand why this might upset family members – because you don't mean any harm by it at all. You will go to the ends of the earth to help or support a parent or sibling, but at the same time you take delight in controversy and are not above winding up brothers and sisters just for the pure fun of it – although you would say it's educational for them, and that you're just playing devil's advocate. You are not confrontational and will not outright defy a parent's authority, but you always manage to find creative ways of bending rules you don't enjoy. Independence is very important to you, and you may choose to stick to certain rules, but that would be because you want to, not because you have to. Not remotely territorial, you're happy to share your bedroom with an open door policy, positively welcoming others who want to admire your eclectic tastes in furnishings and decoration!

As a sister, you are: Quirky, individual, philosophical
Reacting to parental authority, you are: Inventive, independent
Your family strengths: Eccentricity, humanitarianism
Your family weakness: Controversialist tendency
Working with Your Aquarius Moon at Home: Try these journal

prompts on your Moon at Home sheet.

- How much do you agree or disagree with the description of your Aquarius Moon at home? Remember, the Moon is the energy of how you feel, so even if you don't behave exactly as described, is it how you'd *like* to behave?
- Think of a time when your own quirkiness or individuality has helped a sibling to be themselves, or perhaps a time when you've been able to handle a family drama in a laid back, philosophical manner. Does your humanitarian streak have a positive impact on the family?
- Conversely, remember a time when your unpredictable moods have caused problems for other family members. Does their never quite knowing how you will react mean that brothers and sisters have to be cautious around you? What about the last time you provoked a family member with deliberately controversial words or actions. How did that work out? How might you use the strengths of your Aquarius Moon to stay true to yourself but be less provocative next time?

The Pisces Moon at Home

Gentle, dreamy and oh, so sensitive, you are in many ways the soul of the home, nurturing all family members even at the expense of your own needs and wants. You will take on board the triumphs and despairs of brothers and sisters as though they were your own, feeling exceptionally deeply for them at all times. Your sensitivity does mean that you are incredibly easily hurt, however, and siblings may be impatient with you taking everything to heart so much. More than most Moon Signs, you do actually need those parental boundaries, because you're not the most responsible of people. You don't mean to be irresponsible, but you just get lost in your own little world and forget what you're supposed to be doing. During major family decisions, you'll plump for the idealistic option no matter what, and no matter how unrealistic. You are a compassionate daughter and sister, but you would rather resort to telling white lies than face difficult situations head on, which does mean that sometimes sibling rivalry or feuds spiral out of control instead of being dealt with at an early stage. When things do go badly at home, your mood of deep despair is very tough to break through.

As a sister, you are: Supportive, idealistic, spiritual

Reacting to parental authority, you are: Irresponsible, not always honest

Your family strengths: Sensitivity, compassion

Your family weakness: Unrealism

Working with Your Pisces Moon at Home: Try these journal prompts on your Moon at Home sheet.

- How much do you agree or disagree with the description of your Pisces Moon at home? Remember, the Moon is the energy of how you feel, so even if you don't behave exactly as described, is it how you'd *like* to behave?
- Think of a time when you have been able to support a sibling through a tough time, or offer them or your parents some spiritual insight. How has your sensitivity made the home a more nurturing place to be? Do others come to rely on your compassionate nature? Who do you turn to when you need compassion?
- Conversely, remember a time when you behaved irresponsibly, knowingly or not, and caused anxiety to your parents. Were you honest or dishonest about the situation? What about a time when your unrealistic expectations placed pressure on your family or when you were unable to accept the reality of a family problem? How might you use the strengths of your Pisces Moon to deal with these situations differently next time?

Your 12 Home Moods

As the Moon progresses through the 12 houses each month, your mood at home will subtly change. You will always remain true to your Moon Sign – so a deep and meaningful Scorpio Moon sister isn't suddenly going to turn into an easy-going Libra Moon socialite sister, but within the background flavour that your Moon Sign provides, your focus will shift.

Home Moon Transiting 1st House

You're very sensitive to the moods and feelings of family members and this is generally a warm and sympathetic few days at home. However, if you have something you want to say, or you feel that you need some extra attention, these energies can be pretty demanding and you might create a scene of a drama.

Home Moon Transiting 2nd House

It's all about your personal space and your personal stuff during this transit. You'll react emotionally to anyone borrowing something of yours or invading your room. You'll also be more troubled than normal by rows between parents, because these cut to the heart of your sense of security.

Home Moon Transiting 3rd House

You take your family for granted during this transit and have casual, light conversations at home instead of the deep and meaningful ones. Generally a cheerful, fluffy time but the superficiality can annoy you if you know there is something which needs addressing.

Home Moon Transiting 4th House

This is the homebody transit and home and family will be dramatically more important to you than normal for a couple of days. There are nostalgic and sentimental energies at work too and it can be an emotional time when growing up gets in the way of wanting to stay a child.

Home Moon Transiting 5th House

A brilliant time for beautifying your room with homemade bits and bobs, decorating or enjoying traditional family fun. There's a light-hearted energy at play and laughter is a very healing way to defuse any tensions at home.

Home Moon Transiting 6th House

Clean, tidy and sort during this super organised transit. Dredge stuff out from under your bed and give your hard-working parents a hand. If there's a domestic goddess lurking anywhere in you, however well hidden she is, she'll show up now.

Home Moon Transiting 7th House

Any conflicts at home will be magnified under this transit, simply because you care so much. At a time of raised emotions, everything is either fantastic or horrific, and jealousy or envy towards siblings can push all the wrong buttons.

Home Moon Transiting 8th House

You'll be more selfish and possessive than normal under this transit, and may react negatively to any changes at home. Power struggles with parents are common and you'll want to be given an extremely good reason for listening to any opinion other than your own.

Home Moon Transiting 9th House

Drag your family out of a rut during this transit. It's the perfect time for pointing out that "because we always do it this way" isn't a reason to not try something new. You're potentially very inspirational to younger brothers and sisters at this time too.

Home Moon Transiting 10th House

If you're not keeping up with the Joneses, you'll be desperate to do so under this transit. You're very concerned about what other people will think of your home, your family, your room… and that can make you more shallow than normal.

Home Moon Transiting 11th House

Never mind your family, it's your friends that are your top priority under this transit. It can be a brilliant, busy time at home with lots of comings and goings with your mates… but your family might be irritated that you're treating the place like a hotel.

Home Moon Transiting 12th House

You'll be extra moody and extra wistful during this transit, which could be a good or bad thing, depending on the mood of other family members. At its best, this is a beautifully creative and soulful time at home. At its worst, you'll despair of the people you live with and hope to abscond on a luxury liner sometime soon.

Exercise: Tracking Your Home Moods

Find out which house your moon is transiting today. How does that match up with what you've experienced at home today? Remember to blend in the overall energies of your Moon Sign too. If you can track this every day for one whole moon cycle – 28 days – then at the end of that cycle you'll start to notice patterns repeating. Use the downloadable Moon at Home journal page to keep track, or just make notes in your journal as you go along.

Examples:

Aries Moon personality when the Home Moon is transiting the 2nd House – your competitive streak will emerge over who's got the biggest bedroom or the newest gadgets among you and your siblings, and it will really upset you to lose any of those battles. On the other hand, you'll be happy to accept a "bribe" by parents in order to accept a rule you would otherwise have contended.

Gemini Moon Personality when the Home Moon is transiting the 9th House – your boredom levels go through the roof but you can use all of your persuasive charm to shake things up a little bit, perhaps getting parents to agree to a new routine, a swap of rooms or even a house move.

Scorpio Moon personality when the Home Moon is transiting the 4th House – you'll be intensely emotional over family issues and possibly a little tearful about getting older or watching a sibling grow up. Care is needed to avoid this emotion spilling over into confrontation with people who are completely blameless for the passage of time.

Using the Moon to Help with Home Issues and Decisions

As well as tracking the Moon's movements through your chart and understanding how this can affect your moods and attitude at home, you can also be more proactive with using the Moon's energies. For most common situations, there are some lunar energies, signs and houses which are more helpful than others, and if you have the chance to plan ahead it helps to know which days might be best for handling certain things. Of course you won't always have a choice, but when you do, try to choose the following moon transits and energies when you:

Announce that you've turned vegetarian – moon in either humanitarian Aquarius or idealistic Sagittarius, moon transiting your 3rd House (if they won't mind) or 1st House (if they will).

Introduce a new boyfriend – moon in Pisces (for romance) or Capricorn (for maturity), moon transiting your 5th or 7th House.

Makeover your bedroom – moon in stylish Libra, moon transiting your 4th or 5th House.

Argue your case for being allowed to go somewhere or do something – moon in lovably eccentric Aquarius or responsible Virgo, moon transiting your 1st or 9th House.

Hold a party at home – Moon in sociable Gemini or charming Libra, moon transiting your 11th or 5th House.

Tell your family that you're gay – Moon in straightforward Sagittarius or nurturing Cancer, moon transiting your 1st House.

Tell your family that you're in trouble at school – Moon in Virgo (for honesty) or Pisces (for understanding), moon transiting your 3rd, 4th or 6th House.

Confide in your family that you're being bullied – Moon in Aquarius (for righteous indignation) or in Pisces (for compassion), moon transiting your 1st or 8th House.

Explain to your family that you don't want to follow the career or educational path they want you to follow – Moon in confident Aries or Leo, moon transiting your 10th House.

Confess something to a sibling – Moon in generous Leo or light-hearted Gemini, moon transiting your 3rd House.

Confide to a parent your worries about a sibling – Moon in mature Taurus or Capricorn, moon transiting your 6th or 7th House.

Babysit (siblings or others) – Moon in Cancer (for patience) or Capricorn (for maturity), moon transiting your 4th or 5th House.

Defuse sibling rivalry – Moon in happy go lucky Gemini or diplomatic Libra, moon transiting your 5th or 9th House.

(All purpose) tell the family something important which they won't like to hear – Moon in Aries (for bravery) or Taurus (for emotional stability), moon transiting your 4th House.

Don't panic if the "right" Moon Sign or house transit doesn't fit with what you need or want to do! Any tasks, at any time, will be easier to manage if you refer back to what you already know about your lunar personality and its strengths and weaknesses, both at home and in everyday life. If you have to do something awkward or difficult on a day when the Moon Sign or house transit isn't ideal, find out which sign the Moon will be in on that day, and which of your houses it will be transiting. Think carefully about the energies in play – what can you do to make the most of the Moon's energies, and to minimise any particular problems?

Chapter 7

Your Friendship Moon

Friendships are important to all humans – we are by nature sociable creatures, although some of us are happy with just one or two close friends, while others like to surround themselves with dozens of people. Our choice of friends says a lot about us. Do you like friends who challenge you and stretch your limits, or friends who tell you what you want to hear? Friends who are the lives and souls of the party, or those who let you shine stronger than they do? Studious, serious friends or friends who always put fun first? The truest friendships are those where friends either have a lot in common or where they bring out the best in one another.

It is absolutely not the case that some signs (Moon, Sun, Ascendant or anything else) "get on" and some don't; or that such and such a sign is doomed to not like such and such another sign. Astrological compatibility is very complex and involves the whole of both charts. It is, however, possible to make generalisations about which personalities are most likely to "click" with one another, all other things being equal. But if your best friend's Sun or Moon Sign doesn't match what I say here is your perfect friend, don't dump them! It's likely that there are other parts of her chart which "fit" well with yours. If the relationship is working well, leave it be, and don't ever take those kinds of decisions based purely on astrology alone! Now, that warning made, let's find out how your lunar personality and the transits of the Moon have an influence on your social life. You can use the Friendship Moon journal sheet to work through this chapter (downloadable from the website) or you can create your own journal pages.

The Aries Friendship Moon

Among any given group of friends, the Aries lunar personality is likely to be the outright leader. Your very strong views (on just about everything!) are not open to debate and you are perhaps the least likely of all the lunar signs to fall victim to peer pressure – you're more likely to be applying the pressure, even unconsciously, to others. Impulsive behaviour can end up getting not only you into trouble (or even danger), but your friends too. You are courageous in support and protection of those you care for, but you do have a somewhat alarming temper, which can really hurt. Because you think and act so quickly, you don't always care if what you say upsets someone, so if a friend is similarly volatile, it can be a rocky road. To your credit, however, you're also very quick to apologise and you do try hard to make up for your mistakes. When it comes to making new friends, you find it relatively easy, but your direct approach can be intimidating to more reticent personalities. Typically you do have a reasonably large circle of friends, but your independent nature can cope with periods of fewer friendships too.

Sociability rating (how much you like to be around others and how easy you find it to interact): 8/10

Likelihood of bending to peer pressure: 2/10

Friendship strengths: Courage, dynamism

Friendship weaknesses: Impetuosity, temper

What you need from a friendship: Someone who isn't offended by your temper and can help ground your more risky behaviours

Best friend material: (Sun, Moon or Ascendant in) ambitious Capricorn

Least likely to gel with: (Sun, Moon or Ascendant in) moody Cancer

Working with Your Aries Friendship Moon: Try these journal prompts on your Friendship Moon sheet.

- Do you recognise this description of you as a friend? Ask a friend how she views you and whether she recognises the description – she probably will, even if you don't! Look at your friend's Friendship Moon description too. Do you recognise her there? How do you think you both interact via your lunar energies?

- Think about the courage and dynamism you bring to your friendship group. Can you think of any examples of these qualities of yours in action? How about your impetuousness and temper – how do these affect your friendships? Is there a way in which you can use the strengths of your Aries Moon to widen your social circle, or to strengthen your existing friendships?

The Taurus Friendship Moon

Practical and brim full of common sense, you're the friend that everyone wants when they're facing a crisis. You know how to enjoy yourself, but you also have an inherent sense of wanting to play by the rules, so you rarely lead your mates into trouble – and you can be a definite asset when they need to get out of it. Your stubborn nature is a positive thing when it comes to peer pressure, because you don't give in easily to what others tell you – this offers you a good deal of protection from poor friendship influences too. Being rather emotionally possessive, however, you do hate it when a friend plays away and you take it all very personally. When it comes to making new friends, you're cautious but capable. Never the loudest person in a group, you are nonetheless at ease talking with others, particularly if you have shared interests. You prefer a few close friends to a whole gaggle of acquaintances, because it takes you a while to trust and to open up fully to new people – and having made that investment of trust, they will find that they can depend on you for good.

Sociability rating (how much you like to be around others and how easy you find it to interact): 6/10

Likelihood of bending to peer pressure: 4/10

Friendship strengths: Dependability, loyalty

Friendship weaknesses: Possessiveness, stubbornness

What you need from a friendship: Someone who respects your cautious nature but can add a little spice to your life

Best friend material: (Sun, Moon or Ascendant in) generous Leo

Least likely to gel with: (Sun, Moon or Ascendant in) malleable Libra

Working with Your Taurus Friendship Moon: Try these journal prompts on your Friendship Moon sheet.

- Do you recognise this description of you as a friend? Ask a friend how she views you and whether she recognises the description – she probably will, even if you don't! Look at your friend's Friendship Moon description too. Do you recognise her there? How do you think you both interact via your lunar energies?
- Think about the dependability and loyalty you bring to your friendship group. Can you think of any examples of these qualities of yours in action? How about your possessiveness and stubbornness – how do these affect your friendships? Is there a way in which you can use the strengths of your Taurus Moon to widen your social circle, or to strengthen your existing friendships?

The Gemini Friendship Moon

Ever the social butterfly, you're gregarious, talkative and blessed with ability to mix widely, even charming people with whom you have very little in common. You like to lead conversations and debates among your friends, and find it very hard to keep quiet even if what you have to say isn't likely to be popular. Your restless mind manifests itself in fickle friendship behaviour at times; you don't mean to be unkind; you simply get bored of people very easily and you like to move on. In your heart, you probably fully intend to pay more attention to the temporarily abandoned friend again in the near future, but of course she doesn't see it like that. Although highly intelligent, you do feel the pressure to "fit in" and this, combined with your taste for new things, means that you do sometimes fall victim to peer pressure, against your better judgement. Your emotions are not always easy to handle, so a lot of what you say is relatively superficial but great fun. You don't guard other people's emotions quite so carefully, however, and sometimes you don't think twice before spreading gossip.

Sociability rating (how much you like to be around others and how easy you find it to interact): 10/10

Likelihood of bending to peer pressure: 7/10

Friendship strengths: Fun, humour

Friendship weaknesses: Fickleness, superficiality

What you need from a friendship: Someone who can cope with your flightiness and bring out your hidden depths of emotion

Best friend material: (Sun, Moon or Ascendant in) dreamy Pisces

Least likely to gel with: (Sun, Moon or Ascendant in) intense Scorpio

Working with Your Gemini Friendship Moon: Try these journal prompts on your Friendship Moon sheet.

- Do you recognise this description of you as a friend? Ask a friend how she views you and whether she recognises the description – she probably will, even if you don't! Look at your friend's Friendship Moon description too. Do you recognise her there? How do you think you both interact via your lunar energies?
- Think about the fun and humour you bring to your friendship group. Can you think of any examples of these qualities of yours in action? How about your fickleness and superficiality – how do these affect your friendships?

Is there a way in which you can use the strengths of your Gemini Moon to widen your social circle, or to strengthen your existing friendships?

The Cancer Friendship Moon

You are a warm, sympathetic and nurturing friend, a true shoulder to cry on in times of need and a comfortable, cosy companion when times are good. Your emotions are very close to the surface, so it could be said that you wear your friendship heart well and truly on your sleeve. While this does make you very easily hurt, it also makes others warm to your empathy and honesty. You tend to underestimate how much others like you, and you spend a good deal of your time worrying about friendships, particularly after an argument. It must be said that such arguments are fairly frequent occurrences, since you're both sensitive and moody, and your inexplicable moods can be exasperating to others. Sometimes lacking some self-confidence, you find it hard to stand your ground when you're defending yourself (although much easier if you're defending others), so you do sometimes fall victim to bullying or to unhealthy peer pressure. The presence of a strong family support system, or a strong desire not to upset your family, however, protects you from the worst influences out there. Faced with meeting new people, you feel shy and anxious, but once you pluck up the courage to do so you do make new friends relatively easily.

Sociability rating (how much you like to be around others and how easy you find it to interact): 5/10

Likelihood of bending to peer pressure: 7/10

Friendship strengths: Sympathy, warmth

Friendship weaknesses: Moodiness, oversensitivity

What you need from a friendship: Someone who can rationalise your worries but shares your kind and caring outlook on life

Best friend material: (Sun, Moon or Ascendant in) diplomatic Libra

Least likely to gel with: (Sun, Moon or Ascendant in) arrogant Aries

Working with Your Cancer Friendship Moon: Try these journal prompts on your Friendship Moon sheet.

- Do you recognise this description of you as a friend? Ask a friend how she views you and whether she recognises the description – she probably will, even if you don't! Look at your friend's Friendship Moon description too. Do you recognise her there? How do you think you both interact via your lunar energies?
- Think about the sympathy and warmth you bring to your friendship group. Can you think of any examples of these qualities of yours in action? How about your moodiness and oversensitivity – how do these affect your friendships? Is there a way in which you can use the strengths of your Cancer Moon to widen your social circle, or to strengthen your existing friendships?

The Leo Friendship Moon

A larger than life friend, in the nicest possible way, you are (or strive to be) the undoubted star of your circle. You are warm and generous, both materially and emotionally, and a powerful influence on others. All this sunshine comes at a price, however, and that price is that you demand attention, respect and adoration. When you feel you are not getting enough of any of those things, you can throw tantrums to rival the fiercest two year old. You like to be around others (where else will you get the attention?) so making friends is both easy and essential to you. You do like power, though, and can be guilty of snobbishness or social climbing in who you choose to associate with. Peer pressure is not usually an issue for you, since you're certainly strong enough to carve your own path, but this strong personality can have its drawbacks, with others sometimes finding you arrogant, prideful or pretentious. When friendships are going well, you are a creative, inventive and loyal friend; when they are not going so well, you can be domineering, demanding and a definite show-off.

Sociability rating (how much you like to be around others and how easy you find it to interact): 9/10

Likelihood of bending to peer pressure: 3/10

Friendship strengths: Generosity, creativity

Friendship weaknesses: Snobbishness, pride

What you need from a friendship: Someone who can (gently) bring you down a peg or two when necessary, and who can provide you with some constancy

Best friend material: (Sun, Moon or Ascendant in) stable Taurus

Least likely to gel with: (Sun, Moon or Ascendant in) another attention seeking Leo

Working with Your Leo Friendship Moon: Try these journal prompts on your Friendship Moon sheet.

- Do you recognise this description of you as a friend? Ask a friend how she views you and whether she recognises the description – she probably will, even if you don't! Look at your friend's Friendship Moon description too. Do you recognise her there? How do you think you both interact via your lunar energies?
- Think about the generosity and creativity you bring to your friendship group. Can you think of any examples of these qualities of yours in action? How about your snobbishness and pride – how do these affect your friendships? Is there a way in which you can use the strengths of your Leo Moon to widen your social circle, or to strengthen your existing friendships?

The Virgo Friendship Moon

Emotionally quite shy and reserved, it takes a lot for you to trust and bond with new friends, so you enjoy having a few close friendships rather than hordes of superficial ones. When you do open up to someone, however, you are a delightfully humorous and modest friend, always willing to help those you care for and full of practical ideas and common sense. You have very high standards in all areas of life and you are discriminating in your choice of friends, preferring to be alone rather than with those who don't quite make the cut. These high standards generally keep you out of trouble, but they do make life difficult for those who are in your inner circle, because your nature is to criticise. To be fair, you criticise yourself just as much, if not more, than you criticise your friends, but still – the perfectionist inside you can annoy others. Although your common sense stops you doing anything silly, you do worry about not fitting in and you fight a constant battle between giving in to peer pressure and maintaining your own individuality. When it comes to making new friends, you find the whole process intimidating and nerve racking; you would much rather stay with the status quo.

Sociability rating (how much you like to be around others and how easy you find it to interact): 3/10

Likelihood of bending to peer pressure: 5/10

Friendship strengths: Helpfulness, modesty

Friendship weaknesses: Shyness, critical nature

What you need from a friendship: Someone who can boost your confidence and appreciate your deeper qualities

Best friend material: (Sun, Moon or Ascendant in) open-minded Sagittarius

Least likely to gel with: (Sun, Moon or Ascendant in) aloof Aquarius

Working with Your Virgo Friendship Moon: Try these journal prompts on your Friendship Moon sheet.

- Do you recognise this description of you as a friend? Ask a friend how she views you and whether she recognises the description – she probably will, even if you don't! Look at your friend's Friendship Moon description too. Do you recognise her there? How do you think you both interact via your lunar energies?

- Think about the helpfulness and modesty you bring to your friendship group. Can you think of any examples of these qualities of yours in action? How about your shyness and critical nature – how do these affect your friendships? Is there a way in which you can use the strengths of your Virgo Moon to widen your social circle, or to strengthen your existing friendships?

The Libra Friendship Moon

Sociable, refined and graceful, you are much loved by your friends for your style, tact and sophistication. Your instinctive need for balance and harmony turns you into a peacemaker and diplomat extraordinaire, who can always be relied upon to smooth over arguments and heal social wounds. You are naturally kind and an excellent listener, but your need for people to like you means that you are often guilty of saying or doing what you think someone wants to hear or see, rather than being true to yourself. The need to fit in is strong too, and you are perhaps one of the most likely of all of the lunar signs to be swayed by peer pressure, particularly since you are easily led and desperate to avoid alienating existing friends. When making new friends you are relaxed and open and able to put others at their ease; consequently you have the rare ability to make friends with barely a thought – people just want to be around you. In a crisis you are calm and rational, so you're a wonderful friend to have around in both good times and bad – provided you tell the truth and avoid becoming too dependent on your friends.

Sociability rating (how much you like to be around others and how easy you find it to interact): 10/10

Likelihood of bending to peer pressure: 8/10

Friendship strengths: Diplomacy, kindness

Friendship weaknesses: Easily led, overly eager to please

What you need from a friendship: Someone who loves your social graces but can show you a deeper and more honest way to relate

Best friend material: (Sun, Moon or Ascendant in) nurturing Cancer

Least likely to gel with: (Sun, Moon or Ascendant in) stick in the mud Taurus

Working with Your Libra Friendship Moon: Try these journal prompts on your Friendship Moon sheet.

- Do you recognise this description of you as a friend? Ask a friend how she views you and whether she recognises the description – she probably will, even if you don't! Look at your friend's Friendship Moon description too. Do you recognise her there? How do you think you both interact via your lunar energies?
- Think about the diplomacy and kindness you bring to your friendship group. Can you think of any examples of these qualities of yours in action? How about your tendency to say what others want to hear, or your willingness to follow peer pressure – how do these affect your friendships? Is there a way in which you can use the strengths of your Libra Moon to widen your social circle, or to strengthen your existing friendships?

The Scorpio Friendship Moon

Emotionally intense, passionate and secretive, you bore very fast of the normal, superficial social interactions we all take for granted, and you long for a more meaningful connection with your friends. Others find you intriguing and mysterious, and for the lucky few who are allowed to become close to you, you are an endless source of inspiration and insight. You are a jealous friend, however, and prone to overreacting when you feel wronged. With a temper to rival even Moon in Aries personalities, you know how to wound and you're not afraid to do so, harbouring grudges for a long time. You underestimate your own emotional power, and can sometimes, albeit inadvertently, end up in the role of bully, as others are intimidated by you and you are irritated by that. When you want to make new friends, you can do so with relative ease, but you refuse to be forced into social situations not of your own choosing, and can be quite a loner. You're more than happy with your own company, and don't feel the need for friendships just for the sake of having friendships – there has to be something in particular which attracts you to a friend, otherwise the relationship will remain, from your side, at arm's length.

Sociability rating (how much you like to be around others and how easy you find it to interact): 2/10

Likelihood of bending to peer pressure: 2/10

Friendship strengths: Intrigue, insight

Friendship weaknesses: Jealousy, vengefulness

What you need from a friendship: Someone who shares your powers of perception and can help you lighten up a little

Best friend material: (Sun, Moon or Ascendant in) eccentric Aquarius

Least likely to gel with: (Sun, Moon or Ascendant in) superficial Gemini

Working with Your Scorpio Friendship Moon: Try these journal prompts on your Friendship Moon sheet.

- Do you recognise this description of you as a friend? Ask a friend how she views you and whether she recognises the description – she probably will, even if you don't! Look at your friend's Friendship Moon description too. Do you recognise her there? How do you think you both interact via your lunar energies?

- Think about the mystery and insight you bring to your friendship group. Can you think of any examples of these qualities of yours in action? How about your jealousy and vengefulness – how do these affect your friendships? Is there a way in which you can use the strengths of your Scorpio Moon to widen your social circle, or to strengthen your existing friendships?

The Sagittarius Friendship Moon

A positive, enthusiastic and energetic friend. You tell it like it is. Your personality is open and honest, and friends appreciate that with you, what they see is definitely what they get. Hugely optimistic, you always think the best of others, and of situations – but this optimism is not always backed by common sense, and recklessness can be an issue for you, made worse by the fact that friends tend to follow your (not always brilliant) example. You enjoy a typically large circle of friends and your approachable, friendly nature makes it easy for you to get to know others. You don't like to be tied down, however, and will resent any attempts by a friend to stop you seeing other people or pursuing other interests. You give others plenty of space to be themselves, and you demand and expect nothing less in return. Peer pressure issues for you are not so much about fitting in, because you don't care whether you do or not, but more about daring to do new things or break new barriers, sometimes with disastrous results. Philosophical through and through, however, you don't tend to learn a lesson from this, and will cheerfully move on to the next fun but "iffy" situation.

Sociability rating (how much you like to be around others and how easy you find it to interact): 7/10

Likelihood of bending to peer pressure: 7/10

Friendship strengths: Optimism, honesty

Friendship weaknesses: Recklessness, much independence needed

What you need from a friendship: Someone who won't box you in but can bring common sense to blend with your optimism

Best friend material: (Sun, Moon or Ascendant in) helpful Virgo

Least likely to gel with: (Sun, Moon or Ascendant in) needy Pisces

Working with Your Sagittarius Friendship Moon: Try these journal prompts on your Friendship Moon sheet.

- Do you recognise this description of you as a friend? Ask a friend how she views you and whether she recognises the description – she probably will, even if you don't! Look at your friend's Friendship Moon description too. Do you recognise her there? How do you think you both interact via your lunar energies?
- Think about the optimism and openness you bring to your friendship group. Can you think of any examples of these qualities of yours in action? How about your recklessness and your need for independence – how do these affect your friendships? Is there a way in which you can use the strengths of your Sagittarius Moon to widen your social circle, or to strengthen your existing friendships?

The Capricorn Friendship Moon

Hard-working, practical and grounded, you are a "salt of the earth" friend, able to pick up and dust down others and set them back on the right path in a heartbeat. You're the one who knows what to do in a crisis and will remain unflappable, no matter what. Outward appearances can be deceptive, however, and despite your in control exterior, you are surprisingly insecure at heart. You don't show your emotions easily, even to close friends, which means they often cannot help you because they don't know how you feel, which is a great shame. You cover up hurts with laughter, so you are good fun to be around, but for true happiness you need to trust someone very deeply indeed.

Preoccupied with status, you are vulnerable to the materialistic types of peer pressure, to have the latest gadgets and the coolest designer wear, but your common sense guards you against getting involved with reckless behaviour. Making new friends can be a challenge for you as you find it so hard to reveal who you really are. As a result, you are careful to nurture your existing friendships well, and you do tend to form very long lasting friendships which will survive innumerable ups and downs.

Sociability rating (how much you like to be around others and how easy you find it to interact): 5/10

Likelihood of bending to peer pressure: 6/10

Friendship strengths: Practical nature, wisdom

Friendship weaknesses: Inner reserve, insecurity

What you need from a friendship: Someone with the power and warmth to break through your barriers

Best friend material: (Sun, Moon or Ascendant in) inspirational Aries

Least likely to gel with: (Sun, Moon or Ascendant in) another reserved Capricorn

Working with Your Capricorn Friendship Moon: Try these journal prompts on your Friendship Moon sheet.

- Do you recognise this description of you as a friend? Ask a friend how she views you and whether she recognises the description – she probably will, even if you don't! Look at your friend's Friendship Moon description too. Do you recognise her there? How do you think you both interact via your lunar energies?
- Think about the practical skills and wisdom you bring to your friendship group. Can you think of any examples of these qualities of yours in action? How about your inner reserve and insecurities – how do these affect your friendships? Is there a way in which you can use the strengths of

your Capricorn Moon to widen your social circle, or to strengthen your existing friendships?

The Aquarius Friendship Moon

Eccentric, quirky and highly individualistic, you are a complicated friend – on the one hand, people find you fascinating, but on the other hand, you don't want anyone getting too close. You find it tricky to "do" emotions and you'd rather discuss politics with your mates than delve into how you really feel about a family row or your latest crush. Privacy is very important to you and even your closest friends sometimes wonder if they really know you at all. You are very kind, however, and will always do your best to help your friends, although your idealistic solutions are often not that practical in real life. Making new friends isn't an issue for you as such, since you don't spend a lot of time worrying about how many friends you do or do not have – you don't court popularity and are almost completely immune from peer pressure. The friendships you do have are often unconventional in some way, or disapproved of by others – and the more that is the case, the more deeply involved you will become. Something of an enigma, those who do make it into your inner sanctum will find a fun, inventive and certainly never boring friend.

Sociability rating (how much you like to be around others and how easy you find it to interact): 3/10

Likelihood of bending to peer pressure: 2/10

Friendship strengths: Idealism, originality

Friendship weaknesses: Aloofness, unwillingness to reveal emotions

What you need from a friendship: Someone who can help you channel your emotions and who won't give up until they find the real you

Best friend material: (Sun, Moon or Ascendant in) insightful Scorpio

Least likely to gel with: (Sun, Moon or Ascendant in) private Virgo

Working with Your Aquarius Friendship Moon: Try these journal prompts on your Friendship Moon sheet.

- Do you recognise this description of you as a friend? Ask a friend how she views you and whether she recognises the description – she probably will, even if you don't! Look at your friend's Friendship Moon description too. Do you recognise her there? How do you think you both interact via your lunar energies?
- Think about the idealism and originality you bring to your friendship group. Can you think of any examples of these qualities of yours in action? How about your aloofness and unwillingness to reveal emotions – how do these affect your friendships? Is there a way in which you can use the strengths of your Aquarius Moon to widen your social circle, or to strengthen your existing friendships?

The Pisces Friendship Moon

Your friends know you as a sensitive, ethereal girl with a mystical, otherworldly aura about her. Your compassion is legendary and you will willingly sacrifice your own best interests to help a friend, never expecting anything in return. Unfortunately, your ability to soak up the worries of others doesn't do a lot for your own mental health, and you are very easily stressed out, especially when one or more of your mates is also going through a difficult patch. Your intuition is exceptionally strong and you quickly form a psychic link with those you care for, anticipating their words and deeds with ease, which can be both a blessing and a curse. Easily pressurised into doing things you wouldn't ordinarily do, you find it hard to stand your ground against bullying or peer pressure, although your imagination and dreamy nature do help you to step away from the real world when it all gets a bit much. That imagination is a bit of a double-edged sword too, though, and can lead to you telling lies to your friends in order to avoid confrontation. You strongly believe that honesty is not always the best policy, but not all of your friends would agree.

Sociability rating (how much you like to be around others and how easy you find it to interact): 5/10

Likelihood of bending to peer pressure: 8/10

Friendship strengths: Intuition, compassion

Friendship weaknesses: Dishonesty, low stress threshold

What you need from a friendship: Someone who can apply logic to your wilder worries but a healthy dose of humour to counteract your stress

Best friend material: (Sun, Moon or Ascendant in) airy Gemini

Least likely to gel with: (Sun, Moon or Ascendant in) blunt Sagittarius

Working with Your Pisces Friendship Moon: Try these journal prompts on your Friendship Moon sheet.

- Do you recognise this description of you as a friend? Ask a friend how she views you and whether she recognises the description – she probably will, even if you don't! Look at your friend's Friendship Moon description too. Do you recognise her there? How do you think you both interact via your lunar energies?
- Think about the intuition and compassion you bring to your friendship group. Can you think of any examples of these qualities of yours in action? How about your tendency to lie and your super high stress levels – how do these affect your friendships? Is there a way in which you can use the strengths of your Pisces Moon to widen your social circle, or to strengthen your existing friendships?

Your 12 Friendship Moods

As the Moon progresses through the 12 houses each month, your mood towards your friends will subtly change. You will always remain true to your Moon Sign – so a gregarious Leo Moon personality isn't suddenly going to turn into a reticent Virgo Moon personality, but within the background flavour that your Moon Sign provides, your focus will shift.

Friendship Moon Transiting 1st House

It's all about you during this transit – what you want, what you need, what you expect. You'll be more selfish than usual, and less willing to accommodate the wishes of friends. Leading your social group will come easily, however, and if you can keep your demands under control, it can be a memorable few days.

Friendship Moon Transiting 2nd House

Fitting in with the group is very important now as it gives you a sense of security. If that's lacking, you'll try hard to win approval, at whatever cost. Being on the outside looking in distresses you during this transit.

Friendship Moon Transiting 3rd House

A happy, friendly, chatty transit, great for sharing gossip and for spending hours just "being" with your friends and enjoying their company. With your communication skills shining, it's a great time for reaching out and making new friends too.

Friendship Moon Transiting 4th House

Your home and family are central to this transit. Having friends round to yours fills you with delight, but if your family and friends don't get on this can be a few days filled with anxiety and a conflict of loyalties.

Friendship Moon Transiting 5th House

Laughter, fun and creative activities are the order of the day and you'll love getting together with friends to "make" or "do" stuff. It's a very flirtatious time too; you mean it all as harmless fun, but watch out for fireworks if a friend thinks you're getting a bit too friendly with her crush.

Friendship Moon Transiting 6th House

Perfect for planning group trips or sharing homework or revision sessions. You're taking life seriously under this transit and could clash with a friend who wants to mess about instead of getting on with the business in hand.

Friendship Moon Transiting 7th House

How you relate to one person in particular comes under the spotlight during this transit. It can be a wonderful time for forging a new friendship… or a dramatic time as one ends. The strengths and weaknesses of your friendship are fully exposed.

Friendship Moon Transiting 8th House

Revenge, betrayal, power struggles – it's all here. Dramatic, scheming energies make this couple of days a potential minefield for friendships, with everyone taking things very personally and being unlikely to forgive and forget all that easily.

Friendship Moon Transiting 9th House

If you're bored with a friend, it will be hard to hide it during this transit. An intellectual match is important just now and you'll feel uneasy if your friend is well below or above your own standard in that respect. You're being challenged to find common ground so that you can share some new experiences.

Friendship Moon Transiting 10th House

Who's the leader of the pack? Who has the coolest clothes? Who's getting the best marks at school? Who's getting the most admiring glances? This is a highly competitive transit and you'll be constantly comparing yourself to your mates – and if you're not coming out on top, your mood will suffer.

Friendship Moon Transiting 11th House
The most gregarious transit of all, and the perfect time to consciously choose to meet new people. You can really spread your social wings under this transit and you'll be much more confident than normal. Getting involved with purposeful groups like charities or sports teams is especially favoured now.

Friendship Moon Transiting 12th House
A sentimental transit, good for letting your friends know exactly how much you care about them. Emotions are running high and sensitivity is the name of the game. A good transit for reconciliations and for heart to heart talks.

Exercise: Tracking Your Friendship Moods

Find out which house your moon is transiting today. How does that match up with what you've experienced with your friends today? Remember to blend in the overall energies of your Moon Sign too. If you can track this every day for one whole moon cycle – 28 days – then at the end of that cycle you'll start to notice patterns repeating. Use the downloadable Moon Friendship journal page to keep track, or just make notes in your journal as you go along.

Examples:

Capricorn Moon personality when the Friendship Moon is transiting the 10th House – your competitive streak is exceptionally strong now and you'll feel anxious and stressed if you're not being or having "the best" among your group of friends. You'll need to work hard to avoid this spilling over into resentment or sulkiness, which your friends won't understand,

and which is hardly fair.

Aquarius Moon personality when the Friendship Moon is transiting the 12th House – it's much easier for you to express your emotions now, so you can choose this time to apologise to a friend you have upset… or explain to someone how they have upset you.

Libra Moon personality when the Friendship Moon is transiting the 6th House – you're highly organised under this transit and you'll find it easier to convince a group of friends to pull together to get homework or coursework out of the way, so that you can relax together later.

Using the Moon to Help with Your Social Life

As well as tracking the Moon's movements through your chart and understanding how this can affect your moods and attitude towards friends, you can also be more proactive with using the Moon's energies. For most common situations, there are some lunar energies, signs and houses which are more helpful than others, and if you have the chance to plan ahead it helps to know which days might be best for handling certain things. Of course you won't always have a choice, but when you do, try to choose the following moon transits and energies when you:

Want to meet new friends – Moon in gregarious Gemini or sociable Libra, moon transiting your 3rd or 11th House.

Tackle a sensitive issue with a friend – Moon in Libra (for tact) or Pisces (for compassion), Moon transiting 1st or 7th House.

Want to be more confident in a group – Moon in assertive Aries or jovial Sagittarius, Moon transiting your 1st or 11th House.

Hold a party at home – Moon in sociable Gemini or charming Libra, moon transiting your 11th or 5th House.

Plan a party, not at home – Moon in Virgo (for organisation) or Libra (for social skills), Moon transiting your 9th or 11th House.

Want to break off a friendship – Moon in confident Leo or airy

Gemini, Moon transiting your 7th or 8th House.

Stand up to a bully – Moon in Scorpio (for defiance), Aquarius (for justice) or Aries (for bravery), Moon transiting your 1st or 8th House.

Cheer up a friend – Moon in nurturing Cancer or good-humoured Leo, Moon transiting your 3rd or 5th House.

Confide a secret to a friend – Moon in emotional Pisces or free speaking Gemini, Moon transiting your 1st or 12th House.

Keep someone's secret safe – Moon in Taurus (for dependability), Cancer (for loyalty) or Scorpio (for secrecy), Moon transiting your 12th House.

Reveal a secret in a friend's best interests – Moon in Capricorn or Virgo, known for their maturity, Moon transiting your 2nd or 7th House.

End malicious gossip – Moon in honest Sagittarius or direct Aries, Moon transiting your 1st or 3rd House.

Lend money or clothes – Moon in generous Leo or practical Virgo, Moon transiting your 6th or 9th House.

Reach out to someone who is lonely or isolated – Moon in Libra (for kindness) or Sagittarius (for joviality), Moon transiting your 3rd or 11th House.

Don't panic if the "right" Moon Sign or house transit doesn't fit with what you need or want to do! Any tasks, at any time, will be easier to manage if you refer back to what you already know about your lunar personality and its strengths and weaknesses, both at home and in everyday life. If you have to do something awkward or difficult on a day when the Moon Sign or house transit isn't ideal, find out which sign the Moon will be in on that day, and which of your houses it will be transiting. Think carefully about the energies in play – what can you do to make the most of the Moon's energies, and to minimise any particular problems?

Chapter 8

Your Moon in Love

Well, they say love makes the world go round, and it's certainly a huge part of your teen years, whether you're completely, madly, dangerously loved up, single and wondering what all the fuss is about or single and wondering what's wrong with you (clue: nothing at all). How does lunar astrology help us understand what goes on when two people get together?

A note about astrological compatibility

As I mentioned briefly in the chapter about **Your Friendship Moon**, there are no hard and fast rules about astrological compatibility. Whether two people fall in love or not, and if they do whether they can sustain that love long term, can be judged relatively accurately from their complete natal charts, but not from any one part of the chart in isolation. It is not true that certain Sun Signs (or Moon Signs, or Ascendant Signs) get on and others don't – we humans are far too complex for that. It is true, however, that some sign energies relate better to other sign energies in a certain situation. So, use this chapter as a guide to love in your teen years, but don't make rash decisions based on anything it says here. If you've fallen for someone listed as "a damp squib" for your Moon Sign – so what? If it's working for you, it's working for you. This is just a guide. And vice versa, if you're having trouble in a relationship with someone listed as a positive match for your Moon Sign – do whatever you need to do to keep yourself healthy and happy, including moving on from the relationship when appropriate.

You might notice that the Moon Signs listed below as a good match for one another are, in fact, what we call "opposite signs".

If you look at the zodiac chart wheel, Aries is opposite Libra, Taurus is opposite Scorpio and so on. In very simple terms, these personalities can be considered opposites too – but, as the well-known cliché tells us, opposites attract. As you grow older, what you want, need and expect from a relationship changes, but as you are just beginning to dip your toe into Cupid's waters, it's often the case that your opposite sign holds almost magnetic attraction for you. Why? Simply because you can see in them, consciously or unconsciously, something which is lacking in you – and they see it likewise when they look at you. Our first attempts at relationships often involve trying to make ourselves whole as we experiment with what it's like to love someone beyond our family and friends, and the opposite sign completes you in a way which is highly attractive. This won't remain the case for ever, and the older you get, the more likely your opposite sign is to be a source of conflict rather than a source of love (remember, though, nobody can do more than make generalisations without whole birth charts to consider) – but for now, those who hold that certain something within themselves which you sense you need are often the ones who make up our first boyfriends and girlfriends.

The sharp eyed among you will also notice that sometimes a sign which is listed here as not being a good match has been listed in the **Your Friendship Moon chapter** as best mate material. What's the deal with that? Surely you either get on or you don't get on? Well – no. It's not always true that a good friendship is the basis for a good relationship. Good friends often become terrible partners, and some of the best partners are people we really wouldn't be friends with if we weren't in love with them. When you're young, especially, it can be the very thing which you'd hate in a relationship which is a good thing for you in a friendship; the very thing which attracts you to a friend would turn you right off them as a partner.

So: stay open-minded and open-hearted, and don't take any

of the sign matches in this book as gospel – they are just a guide, and you're more than welcome to deviate from the map.

All that said: your lunar personality forms the basis of how you relate to others, including how you relate to a boyfriend, or how you feel about being single. Refer back to your lunar personality sheet to remind yourself of your Moon Sign qualities. Let's take a look at this in more detail. You can use the downloadable Your Moon in Love journal sheet to work through this chapter, or you can create your own journal pages.

Your Aries Moon in Love

Why, oh why, you sigh, does it take so long to find love? Permanently in a hurry, your emotions are a whirlwind when it comes to romance. You want a boyfriend now, not next year, and in your enthusiasm you don't always make very wise choices. You want to be the first in your peer group to have a serious relationship and you're quite competitive in love too. You're daring and more than a little bit reckless, and certainly not above getting far too entangled for your own good just because it's exciting. Ironically, you're more than able to be a strong, single girl, and as you get older you will enjoy the independence of singledom for quite some time before you settle down. For now, though, in the tumultuous teen years, you're keen to experience all that there is to experience, and the concept of waiting until you're older just doesn't cross your mind. In a relationship, you're fiery and passionate and you like to be in charge. Prone to bouts of selfishness, you can also be rather thoughtless; many a boy's heart has been broken by an Aries Moon personality who's carelessly said the wrong thing. Since your communication style is open and direct, you don't shy away from talking about sex and other big relationship issues, which is a good thing. Whatever you decide to do, make sure you have all the information you need to keep yourself safe, both physically and emotionally.

What attracts others to you: Your adventurous spirit, no nonsense attitude and fiery passion.

What turns others off: Selfishness, recklessness.

Flirtatiousness rating: 6/10 – you're more likely to simply ask someone out; flirting wastes too much time!

Break up style: You'll just tell him. Bye bye, move on.

A good match – Sun or Moon in: Libra. You benefit from his sense of presence and calm, yet he can match your temper when roused and will stand up to you when you need it.

A damp squib – Sun or Moon in: Cancer. He's much too passive for your adventurous soul, and you have little patience with his worries.

Working with Your Aries Moon in Love: Try these journal prompts on your Moon in Love sheet.

- Write a short pen portrait, without thinking too deeply, of your ideal partner. Not his (or her) looks, but their personality. How does this balance against your own Aries Moon personality? Where would your energies blend well and where would the potential problems be?
- If you have or have had a boyfriend, jot down some key notes about how your relationship worked well, and how (if) it failed. How much did your Aries Moon personality contribute to either of those things? If you know his birth data, find out his Moon Sign and think about how those energies worked with your own lunar personality.
- Consider a time when you were single, including now if appropriate. Are you happy in your single status? Or does it bother you? If you're happy, can you see how the strengths of your Aries Moon are contributing to that? If you're upset or worried about it, can you see why? And how can your Moon Sign strengths help you be stronger as a single individual?

Your Taurus Moon in Love

What's the rush? You're in no particular hurry to find a boyfriend or to be gossiped about by the rest of the school (!) and you're quite cautious when it comes to love and romance. It's not that you don't fancy anyone – on the contrary, you're an active window shopper in Cupid's Mall – but your inner need for security holds you back from taking the leap of faith required to start a new relationship. When you do have a boyfriend, you're an exceptionally loyal partner, if somewhat possessive, and very affectionate in public, and it's crucial that he returns that affection; you can't cope with boys who are all over you in private but shun you when someone's looking. Your stubborn nature tends to hold on to things once you've made that leap, so you'll be slow to end a relationship even if it's going nowhere. Likewise, you won't listen to advice from others, even if they're concerned about your relationship or your choice of partner. When it comes to sex, you're a very practical, responsible girl, and you'll make sure that, should you make that decision, you'll be safe. Patient and rational, however, you won't want to rush into things, and you're certainly capable of standing your ground against a boyfriend who wants to move too fast. Whatever you do or don't get up to in private, however, will stay in private as far as you're concerned. You won't be spilling the beans any time soon, no matter how eager your audience.

What attracts others to you: An inner sensuality, your relaxed attitude and open affection.

What turns others off: Stubbornness, possessiveness.

Flirtatiousness rating: 8/10 – you won't lose your dignity, but flirting at a safe distance indulges your sensual side.

Break up style: Agonisingly long and drawn out. Death by a thousand cuts.

A good match – Sun or Moon in: Scorpio. He can open your eyes to a world beyond the everyday, and help you explore emotions you've kept far too well hidden.

A damp squib – Sun or Moon in: Leo. He's much too showy and arrogant for your taste and his flamboyance disturbs you.

Working with Your Taurus Moon in Love: Try these journal prompts on your Moon in Love sheet.

- Write a short pen portrait, without thinking too deeply, of your ideal partner. Not his (or her) looks, but their personality. How does this balance against your own Taurus Moon personality? Where would your energies blend well and where would the potential problems be?
- If you have or have had a boyfriend, jot down some key notes about how your relationship worked well, and how (if) it failed. How much did your Taurus Moon personality contribute to either of those things? If you know his birth data, find out his Moon Sign and think about how those energies worked with your own lunar personality.
- Consider a time when you were single, including now if appropriate. Are you happy in your single status? Or does it bother you? If you're happy, can you see how the strengths of your Taurus Moon are contributing to that? If you're upset or worried about it, can you see why? And how can your Moon Sign strengths help you be stronger as a single individual?

Your Gemini Moon in Love

Outwardly sociable and very flirtatious, what others don't tend to see is that you are inwardly a little bit afraid of love. A supremely rational sign, the intensity of love scares you, and you will be slow to commit to someone for that reason. You're quite fickle, and will happily go through a number of relatively superficial relationships in a short space of time – perhaps earning yourself an unwelcome reputation along the way. When the right person does come along, however, you make a wonderful partner, fun, lively, intelligent and mischievous. As a single girl, you'll chat endlessly with friends about boys, but you'll find it quite tricky not to worry that there might be something wrong with you if you go through a lengthy patch without a partner. In a relationship, you'll still chat endlessly about how it's going – keeping things private is not your strong point. You're naturally curious about sex and relatively eager to take a relationship to a more intimate stage, but you'll keep your emotions out of it unless and until you're absolutely sure you've chosen the right person. When not a lot is happening on the romance front, you'll enjoy reading or writing about love, following celebrity dating or just living vicariously through a friend's relationship. Your flirtatious nature can upset others though, whether it's your friend who thinks you're being inappropriate with her squeeze, or a current partner who feels insecure because you've always got eyes for someone else.

What attracts others to you: Your intelligence, flirtatiousness and your sociable nature.

What turns others off: Fickleness, too much flirting.

Flirtatiousness rating: 10/10 – if it moves, you'll wiggle your hips and smile coyly at it.

Break up style: Rational and intellectual. You'll give him a list of 327 reasons why it's not working out.

A good match – Sun or Moon in: Sagittarius. He shares your youthful exuberance but helps you add sincerity to your superficiality.

A damp squib – Sun or Moon in: Pisces. His emotional depths frighten you, and he's just not secure enough to cope with your flirting.

Working with Your Gemini Moon in Love: Try these journal prompts on your Moon in Love sheet.

- Write a short pen portrait, without thinking too deeply, of your ideal partner. Not his (or her) looks, but their personality. How does this balance against your own Gemini

Moon personality? Where would your energies blend well and where would the potential problems be?

- If you have or have had a boyfriend, jot down some key notes about how your relationship worked well, and how (if) it failed. How much did your Gemini Moon personality contribute to either of those things? If you know his birth data, find out his Moon Sign and think about how those energies worked with your own lunar personality.
- Consider a time when you were single, including now if appropriate. Are you happy in your single status? Or does it bother you? If you're happy, can you see how the strengths of your Gemini Moon are contributing to that? If you're upset or worried about it, can you see why? And how can your Moon Sign strengths help you be stronger as a single individual?

Your Cancer Moon in Love

Why are all the good ones taken? You're romantic and supremely sensitive, but also very easily hurt. One bad relationship experience is all it takes to turn you off the whole idea for a very long time indeed – and since our first relationships are usually doomed to failure, it follows that Cancer Moon personalities can endure a very patchy love life until at least their early 20s. Security and trust are huge emotional issues for you, and you are not interested in superficial relationships, or in having a boyfriend just for the sake of it, just so that you can say you're not single. Indeed, you are usually perfectly happy when single and secure enough of your own feelings to not be in a rush to follow the crowd. When you do date a boy, it's important to you that people you care about approve of him, which of course, depending how strict or tolerant your family is, can be a bit of a minefield. Ultimately, you will develop the strength to follow your own heart and not worry about the opinions of others, but this will take quite some time. You have an intuitive understanding of the emotional implications of sex and intimacy and you will instinctively protect yourself until you feel very loved by someone. Extremely faithful to and protective of a boyfriend, you can't stand flirting and will react with fury if you feel someone else is getting a little too close to him.

What attracts others to you: Your kindness, dignity and sense of inner security.

What turns others off: Guardedness, seriousness.

Flirtatiousness rating: 2/10 – a very rarely used talent of yours, since you're very conscious of the hurt it can cause.

Break up style: Angst ridden. Was it your fault it's not working? Should you give it one more go? What if he's upset when you tell him?

A good match – Sun or Moon in: Capricorn. He can add some steel to your softness, while never pushing you uncomfortably far beyond your comfort zone.

A damp squib – Sun or Moon in: Aries. He's much too curt and imperious, and his recklessness turns your stomach.

Working with Your Cancer Moon in Love: Try these journal prompts on your Moon in Love sheet.

- Write a short pen portrait, without thinking too deeply, of your ideal partner. Not his (or her) looks, but their personality. How does this balance against your own Cancer Moon personality? Where would your energies blend well and where would the potential problems be?
- If you have or have had a boyfriend, jot down some key notes about how your relationship worked well, and how (if) it failed. How much did your Cancer Moon personality contribute to either of those things? If you know his birth data, find out his Moon Sign and think about how those energies worked with your own lunar personality.
- Consider a time when you were single, including now if appropriate. Are you happy in your single status? Or does

it bother you? If you're happy, can you see how the strengths of your Cancer Moon are contributing to that? If you're upset or worried about it, can you see why? And how can your Moon Sign strengths help you be stronger as a single individual?

Your Leo Moon in Love

How many times a day can one person possibly fall in love? If she has a Leo Moon personality – lots! And you're never just in love; you're overwhelmingly, passionately, desperately in love, or heart-wrenchingly, agonisingly single, because all of your emotions are exaggerated. You're in love with the drama and the sheer romance of, well, being in love, and you like the attention each new relationship brings. You're extremely warm and engaging as a person, and you know it. As you yourself might say, with a trademark trace of arrogance: what's not to love? You certainly attract your fair share of admirers and you dislike being single purely because it doesn't seem as important or glamorous as being "taken". When you are with someone, you're given to grand, romantic gestures, but you're also given to creating a fuss over nothing, so your relationships tend to veer from highs to lows and back again, rarely remaining stable for long. Woe betide him if he doesn't worship you enough, though, because you won't tolerate not being someone's absolute goddess. If he doesn't put you on a pedestal, you're likely to stick the pedestal where it hurts. When it comes to sex and intimate relationships, your passionate nature can't help but be interested – and you do risk getting carried away on the spur of the moment, so you should think carefully about these situations before they happen rather than discovering too late that you've made a terrible mistake.

What attracts others to you: Your joie de vivre, your generosity and your self-confidence.

What turns others off: Arrogance, pomposity.

Flirtatiousness rating: 9/10 – after all, you figure, if you've got it, flaunt it!

Break up style: Dramatic. Often done suddenly and in public, in an Oscar worthy performance.

A good match – Sun or Moon in: Aquarius. His quirkiness teaches you that you don't have to be a drama queen to be loved, and you love that he can always surprise you.

A damp squib – Sun or Moon in: Taurus. He's too busy looking after himself to look after you, and he stubbornly refuses to accept your upper hand in the relationship.

Working with Your Leo Moon in Love: Try these journal prompts on your Moon in Love sheet.

- Write a short pen portrait, without thinking too deeply, of your ideal partner. Not his (or her) looks, but their personality. How does this balance against your own Leo Moon personality? Where would your energies blend well and where would the potential problems be?
- If you have or have had a boyfriend, jot down some key notes about how your relationship worked well, and how (if) it failed. How much did your Leo Moon personality contribute to either of those things? If you know his birth data, find out his Moon sign and think about how those energies worked with your own lunar personality.
- Consider a time when you were single, including now if appropriate. Are you happy in your single status? Or does it bother you? If you're happy, can you see how the strengths of your Leo Moon are contributing to that? If you're upset or worried about it, can you see why? And how can your Moon Sign strengths help you be stronger as a single individual?

Your Virgo Moon in Love

Only the best will do for discriminating Virgo energies, and that goes for love and romance too. You're extremely choosy about who you enter into a relationship with, and definitely prefer to be single than to be with someone you don't really feel for. You hold yourself and others to very high standards of behaviour and you can be quite prim and proper in love. The Edwardian age of chaperones and dating at arms length would have been perfect for you, but alas you live in modern times with all their associated pressures. You do love, and deeply too, but it takes you a long time to really warm to someone, so patience is key when it comes to finding the right partner. You're far more likely to fall in love with someone misunderstood or someone you can help in some way than with the cutest or cleverest boy you know. The earth energies in Virgo mean that you are sensual, and with the right person you will be a highly attentive and affectionate partner, but as a teen the idea of sex is for you fraught with worries over STDs, pregnancy and other practical issues, before you even get to the emotional bit. On the plus side, this does mean that you won't give into pressure to be intimate with someone before you feel ready. Once in a relationship, you are affectionate and warm, but your efforts to "improve" a partner can hurt others, who might feel under constant criticism.

What attracts others to you: Your modesty, intelligence and high standards.

What turns others off: Too much criticism, lack of self-confidence.

Flirtatiousness rating: 5/10 – when you're feeling confident, verbal flirting is a talent of yours, but you'll always remain modest in dress and physical behaviour.

Break up style: The blame game. He didn't do this, he was useless at that… but any part you played in the downfall of the relationship will remain pretty well hidden.

A good match – Sun or Moon in: Pisces. He helps to free your dreams and imagination and tells you that anything is possible with your wealth of talents.

A damp squib – Sun or Moon in: Sagittarius. He's too uncouth, too wild, too scruffy and much, much too frank.

Working with Your Virgo Moon in Love: Try these journal prompts on your Moon in Love sheet.

- Write a short pen portrait, without thinking too deeply, of your ideal partner. Not his (or her) looks, but their personality. How does this balance against your own Virgo Moon personality? Where would your energies blend well and where would the potential problems be?
- If you have or have had a boyfriend, jot down some key notes about how your relationship worked well, and how (if) it failed. How much did your Virgo Moon personality contribute to either of those things? If you know his birth data, find out his Moon Sign and think about how those energies worked with your own lunar personality.
- Consider a time when you were single, including now if appropriate. Are you happy in your single status? Or does it bother you? If you're happy, can you see how the strengths of your Virgo Moon are contributing to that? If you're upset or worried about it, can you see why? And how can your Moon Sign strengths help you be stronger as a single individual?

Your Libra Moon in Love

Oh, the romance! Flowers and rose petals and poetry and rainbows! At least, it is in your head, until you're yanked back to reality and discover that the fluffy stuff is an occasional occurrence (if you're lucky) and that real love is rather more mundane in nature. All the same, you more than any other Moon Sign need a partner in order to feel complete; you just don't feel right being single. So, when it comes to love, you not only wear rose-tinted glasses, but you have all the windows in your house tinted too. You're willing to overlook any/all of his faults if he just stays with you and no, you don't believe that nasty rumour; he wouldn't do that to you. You are easily deceived because you let yourself be deceived; you're also very malleable in a relationship and will bend to his will. All this needn't sound so negative – in a good relationship, you are a fantastic, loving, giving girlfriend – but when you are caught up in a relationship with a strong personality, you can find it hard to extricate yourself, or to ask for help if you need it. Your best protection is to be more discerning about who you choose. You are at risk of agreeing to sex when you don't really want to, purely because you want to be liked. Fortunately, you are an intelligent girl, and having made a mistake once or twice you will learn from it and become stronger – but better yet, don't put yourself in that position to begin with.

What attracts others to you: Your social charm, easy-going nature and your willingness to believe the best of others.

What turns others off: Neediness, unrealistic expectations.

Flirtatiousness rating: 7/10 – your ease in social situations means you end up flirting quite a lot, but almost accidentally and never with malice.

Break up style: Non-existent. You don't do break ups of your own accord. You'll stick it out, even through gritted teeth, until he does the deed himself.

A good match – Sun or Moon in: Aries. He's honest with you and although he has a temper you can more than match his passion.

A damp squib – Sun or Moon in: Capricorn. He could hardly be less romantic and he won't indulge your need not only to be loved but to be made to feel loved.

Working with Your Libra Moon in Love: Try these journal prompts on your Moon in Love sheet.

- Write a short pen portrait, without thinking too deeply, of your ideal partner. Not his (or her) looks, but their personality. How does this balance against your own Libra Moon personality? Where would your energies blend well and where would the potential problems be?

- If you have or have had a boyfriend, jot down some key notes about how your relationship worked well, and how (if) it failed. How much did your Libra Moon personality contribute to either of those things? If you know his birth data, find out his Moon Sign and think about how those energies worked with your own lunar personality.
- Consider a time when you were single, including now if appropriate. Are you happy in your single status? Or does it bother you? If you're happy, can you see how the strengths of your Libra Moon are contributing to that? If you're upset or worried about it, can you see why? And how can your Moon Sign strengths help you be stronger as a single individual?

Your Scorpio Moon in Love

When love bites for a Scorpio Moon, it bites strong and deep. There is no such thing for you as a superficial feeling, or a passing attraction. Your feelings are complicated and intense, and woe betide the person who breaks your heart since you also harbour vengeful tendencies. With a magnetic and somewhat mysterious persona, you rarely go short of admirers, but you do have a tendency to try to control your relationships – it's because of that depth of feeling that you want to make sure nobody hurts you, leading to jealousy and possessiveness which can cause very real problems for your relationships. Being single doesn't bother you; you're perfectly capable of being happy alone for extended periods of time, and you certainly won't consider losing your dignity by chasing after a boy. No, they come to you or not at all. Passionate by nature, you are very interested in sex, almost in a psychological way – for research purposes perhaps! – and you will often be tempted to take a relationship further than might be wise at the time. If you do, however, it will be because you want to, not because you've given in to pressure from him or from your peers. Nor will you be broadcasting the juicy details to all and sundry, because you guard your privacy intensely and tend to be quite secretive about relationships. Your most serious relationships will be distinguished by intense power struggles as you learn how much you can and cannot control, and when to back off – it's a steep learning curve, most definitely, but you'll get there.

What attracts others to you: Your mystique, depth and inherent sensuality.

What turns others off: Jealousy, controlling nature.

Flirtatiousness rating: 2/10 – you simply don't need to flirt, and you find it undignified.

Break up style: Vengeful. You'll never forgive him for what he did to cause the break up. Because of course, it was his fault.

A good match – Sun or Moon in: Taurus. He can stabilise those tumultuous emotions of yours and will match your determination to make the relationship work.

A damp squib – Sun or Moon in: Aquarius. You can't deal with his hidden emotions and his rebelliousness unnerves you.

Working with Your Scorpio Moon in Love: Try these journal prompts on your Moon in Love sheet.

- Write a short pen portrait, without thinking too deeply, of your ideal partner. Not his (or her) looks, but their personality. How does this balance against your own Scorpio Moon personality? Where would your energies blend well and where would the potential problems be?
- If you have or have had a boyfriend, jot down some key notes about how your relationship worked well, and how (if) it failed. How much did your Scorpio Moon personality contribute to either of those things? If you know his birth data, find out his Moon Sign and think about how those energies worked with your own lunar personality.

- Consider a time when you were single, including now if appropriate. Are you happy in your single status? Or does it bother you? If you're happy, can you see how the strengths of your Scorpio Moon are contributing to that? If you're upset or worried about it, can you see why? And how can your Moon Sign strengths help you be stronger as a single individual?

Your Sagittarius Moon in Love

It's not good looks, status, sense of humour or even kindness which you value most in a boyfriend – no, it's that most overlooked of qualities: sincerity. In love, as in other areas of your life, you are totally open and honest, and you expect the same courtesy in return. When you think you can trust a boy, you turn him into a movie idol who can do no wrong – and when he does let you down, your heartbreak is all the greater because of the idealistic way you viewed him before. Nevertheless, you'll pull yourself together quickly and move on to find someone more worthy of your time. Or you might just choose to stay single for a while – you're a very independent girl and you don't need a partner in order to feel complete. You'd like one, sure, because you yearn for someone to share your joy in life, but between relationships you'll be happy enough alone and with your friends. You view sex as another great adventure and something to be enjoyed; this is a very positive and healthy attitude, but it does mean that you sometimes get much deeper into a relationship, much faster, than is necessarily wise. It's not a question of bending to peer pressure though – you just genuinely enjoy new experiences, even (especially?) those which others advise against. You won't be told what to do, so the more parents try to keep you away from someone, the more they will ultimately drive you together, even if you only do it to prove a point.

What attracts others to you: Your optimism, exuberance and your honest, straightforward nature.

What turns others off: Bluntness, restlessness.

Flirtatiousness rating: 8/10 – your cheerful, friendly attitude is easily mistaken for flirting even when you don't intend it, let alone when you do.

Break up style: Friendly. You don't bear grudges, however hurt you are, and will hope to stay on good terms with him.

A good match – Sun or Moon in: Gemini. You appreciate his honesty, intellect and playfulness and he shares your aspirations and passions.

A damp squib – Sun or Moon in: Virgo. He's too uptight and too muted for you, and will take offence too easily when you tell it like it is.

Working with Your Sagittarius Moon in Love: Try these journal prompts on your Moon in Love sheet.

- Write a short pen portrait, without thinking too deeply, of your ideal partner. Not his (or her) looks, but their personality. How does this balance against your own Sagittarius Moon personality? Where would your energies blend well and where would the potential problems be?
- If you have or have had a boyfriend, jot down some key notes about how your relationship worked well, and how (if) it failed. How much did your Sagittarius Moon personality contribute to either of those things? If you know his birth data, find out his Moon Sign and think about how those energies worked with your own lunar personality.
- Consider a time when you were single, including now if appropriate. Are you happy in your single status? Or does it bother you? If you're happy, can you see how the strengths of your Sagittarius Moon are contributing to that? If you're upset or worried about it, can you see why? And how can your Moon Sign strengths help you be stronger as a single individual?

Your Capricorn Moon in Love

Who needs love anyway? You take a slightly aloof, dispassionate view of romance and relationships during your teen years. Although of course you can fall in love as often and as deeply as any other lunar personality, the difference is that you often choose to keep your distance and to love from afar. You fear rejection and hence are reluctant to let anyone through your protective barriers. When you do enter a relationship, you will be a very warm, supportive and loving girlfriend, provided he respects you and treats you well. You are supremely practical and focused, however, and if you think it makes sense to remain single while you concentrate on school or your studies, then you won't hesitate to hang up your "closed to Cupid" sign and stride along as a single with your head held high. Patience and caution are your watch words, and you absolutely will not rush into sex or deep emotional entanglement. As you grow older, you will become (a lot) less cautious in love, but as you start to discover how relationships work, you'll find it all a bit overwhelming and therefore easier left alone. You'll be fascinated by friends' relationships and will learn a lot from the experiences of your friends and siblings, but very often you'll prefer this kind of second-hand romance to the danger and uncertainty of the real thing. Ironically, your fabulous sense of humour and mature approach win you many admirers, and you are an accomplished flirt – it's just that you often choose not to engage deeper than the flirtatious stage.

What attracts others to you: Your humour, your sense of inner wisdom and your older-than-your-years manner.

What turns others off: Diffidence, reluctance to get involved.

Flirtatiousness rating: 7/10 – you could flirt for the nation if you so chose, with humour being your primary weapon.

Break up style: Practical. Your primary concern will be in sorting out the details, taking back possessions, and making alternative arrangements for the time you spent together.

A good match – Sun or Moon in: Cancer. He is warm and kind enough to break through your protection, while remaining dependable and trustworthy.

A damp squib – Sun or Moon in: Libra. He's much too glib for your liking, and he spends far too much time in a fantasy land instead of dealing with reality.

Working with Your Capricorn Moon in Love: Try these journal prompts on your Moon in Love sheet.

- Write a short pen portrait, without thinking too deeply, of your ideal partner. Not his (or her) looks, but their personality. How does this balance against your own Capricorn Moon personality? Where would your energies blend well and where would the potential problems be?
- If you have or have had a boyfriend, jot down some key notes about how your relationship worked well, and how (if) it failed. How much did your Capricorn Moon personality contribute to either of those things? If you know his birth data, find out his Moon Sign and think about how those energies worked with your own lunar personality.
- Consider a time when you were single, including now if appropriate. Are you happy in your single status? Or does it bother you? If you're happy, can you see how the strengths of your Capricorn Moon are contributing to that? If you're upset or worried about it, can you see why? And how can your Moon Sign strengths help you be stronger as a single individual?

Your Aquarius Moon in Love

Never mind the passion, what you're really seeking is a meeting of minds. All that lovey-dovey stuff really isn't your style, but if you find a relationship where he can match your intellect, appreciate your (extensive) opinions and enjoy a feisty debate on the issues which really matter – well then you'll fall head over heels in love. Either that or you'll choose someone society deems completely, totally unsuitable. The more unsuitable the better, in fact. The lunar Aquarius personality in love is a strange and wonderful thing to behold. Your independence and restrained emotions mean that you'll always want and need to retain plenty of freedom in the relationship. At the same time, you'll want to spend as much time as possible close to the amazing guy who's won your attention… and that's an internal conflict you might struggle with. Typically, your need for freedom wins out and can cause the end of many a promising relationship, but you'll barely shed a tear, having more important things to think about. Sex is a curiosity to you but not your major motivation in a relationship. In fact, you're more likely to take a relationship to that level in order to deliberately shock or provoke someone (a parent?) than for your own pleasure. As a girlfriend, even when you are in love, you do find it difficult to express those emotions. One of the most common causes of problems in your relationships is your failure to let him know how much you really do care.

What attracts others to you: Your individuality, your friendliness and your open-minded attitude.

What turns others off: Lack of emotions, high independence.

Flirtatiousness rating: 3/10 – you just can't see the point in flirting, so why bother?

Break up style: Implied. You'll just stop seeing him and expect him to figure it out. Having the actual break up conversation is simply too emotionally awkward for you.

A good match – Sun or Moon in: Leo. You're fascinated by his flair and sense of drama, and his warmth and honesty helps to open up your deeper emotions.

A damp squib – Sun or Moon in: Scorpio. You can't be bothered with the deep and moody stuff and his intense emotions are frankly terrifying for you.

Working with Your Aquarius Moon in Love: Try these journal prompts on your Moon in Love sheet.

- Write a short pen portrait, without thinking too deeply, of your ideal partner. Not his (or her) looks, but their personality. How does this balance against your own Aquarius Moon personality? Where would your energies blend well and where would the potential problems be?
- If you have or have had a boyfriend, jot down some key notes about how your relationship worked well, and how (if) it failed. How much did your Aquarius Moon personality contribute to either of those things? If you know his birth data, find out his Moon Sign and think about how those energies worked with your own lunar personality.
- Consider a time when you were single, including now if appropriate. Are you happy in your single status? Or does it bother you? If you're happy, can you see how the strengths of your Aquarius Moon are contributing to that? If you're upset or worried about it, can you see why? And how can your Moon Sign strengths help you be stronger as a single individual?

Your Pisces Moon in Love

Holding out for a hero? The most romantic and idealistic of all the lunar personalities, you're in love with love itself, highly sensitive and liable to fall in love and out again numerous times a day. Unfortunately, hardly anyone can live up to the knight in shining armour ideal you cherish in your head, so you are invariably disappointed with him once reality sinks in. The key to your romantic happiness is to learn just a tiny bit of realism, without taking away from your beautiful gentleness. Once you learn to love someone for who they are, not who you want them to be, you'll enjoy tremendously satisfying relationships. You are supremely easily hurt, but even after an awful experience you'll get straight back on to the romance merry-go-round; you simply cannot resist it. Your view of sex is as idealistic and romantic as your view of everything else, so a quick fumble simply won't do.

On the plus side, this does protect you to a great extent from rushing into sex with some random boy; it has to be special or you'll withhold your charms until Prince Charming eventually turns up. Your intuition is a powerful tool in your love life, and you should always listen to it; if it tells you something is wrong, then take heed. Try to avoid crying wolf though; when there is a minor niggle in a relationship, you're apt to exaggerate it into being the end of the world – which can quickly push away both boyfriends and friends.

What attracts others to you: Your dreamy nature, gentleness, kindness and grace.

What turns others off: Overly emotional response, too much idealism.

Flirtatiousness rating: 5/10 – it depends on your mood and your motive, but you can flutter your eyelashes with the best of them when you choose to.

Break up style: Traumatic. Cue endless tears and sleepless nights – even when it's your decision to end it.

A good match – Sun or Moon in: Virgo. He helps to ground your emotions and is a true gentleman, unlikely to ever deliberately hurt you.

A damp squib – Sun or Moon in: Gemini. His flirting and fickle nature breaks your heart and he's not able to cope with your depth of emotions.

Working with Your Pisces Moon in Love: Try these journal prompts on your Moon in Love sheet.

- Write a short pen portrait, without thinking too deeply, of your ideal partner. Not his (or her) looks, but their personality. How does this balance against your own Pisces Moon personality? Where would your energies blend well and where would the potential problems be?
- If you have or have had a boyfriend, jot down some key notes about how your relationship worked well, and how

(if) it failed. How much did your Pisces Moon personality contribute to either of those things? If you know his birth data, find out his Moon Sign and think about how those energies worked with your own lunar personality.

- Consider a time when you were single, including now if appropriate. Are you happy in your single status? Or does it bother you? If you're happy, can you see how the strengths of your Pisces Moon are contributing to that? If you're upset or worried about it, can you see why? And how can your Moon Sign strengths help you be stronger as a single individual?

Your 12 Romance Moods

OK, so now you know how your Moon Sign, your lunar personality, colours how you are as a girlfriend and how you are as a strong and sassy single girl. As the Moon progresses through the 12 houses each month, your mood at home will subtly change. You will always remain true to your Moon Sign – so a romantic and idealistic Pisces Moon girl isn't going to morph overnight into a cautious and aloof Capricorn Moon girl, but within the background flavour that your Moon Sign provides, your focus will shift.

Love Moon Transiting 1st House

Flirtatious and outward looking, these are days when it's easy for people to like you and when you make a very good impression on others. A good few days for harmless flirting, and even better for beginning a brand new relationship.

Love Moon Transiting 2nd House

Possessiveness in a relationship can cause trouble now, and you'll have difficulty with anything in love which challenges your sense of security. Not a great time to rock the boat in a relationship, these are nonetheless pleasant days for getting to know someone better and for making any kind of commitment.

Love Moon Transiting 3rd House
It's not easy to be objective about love during this transit, but on the plus side you'll find it easier than normal to express your emotions. Very good for heart to heart talks, and also for talking about love with friends and siblings – and for asking their advice.

Love Moon Transiting 4th House
Family approval for your relationship is uppermost in your mind during this transit and if they don't like your boyfriend, they'll be making that very clear. It's also a nostalgic time and if a relationship has recently broken up, you'll find yourself very emotional as you look back on it.

Love Moon Transiting 5th House
Fun, flirty and slightly reckless, this transit is great for meeting new potential boyfriends, dating, telling someone how you feel about them and generally allowing Cupid to play. It's not an emotionally deep time, however, and feelings may last fleetingly at best.

Love Moon Transiting 6th House
If there are problems in your love life, the stress can affect your health during this transit. Feelings are running high and close to the surface, and distracting you from the general business or day-to-day life. On the other hand, if all is well, you'll positively bloom under this transit, and it's an excellent few days for putting a relationship on a firmer footing; it's also a fine time for cooling one that's blowing too hot.

Love Moon Transiting 7th House
This is the house of love, romance and relationships, and sure enough the Moon's transits through this house bring love to the

forefront of your mind. It's a fantastic transit for deepening a relationship, giving and receiving love, patching up quarrels and enjoying all round togetherness.

Love Moon Transiting 8th House

A difficult few days for relationships, this transit typically enhances jealousy, resentment and anger – but it can also provoke passion of the more enjoyable kind. Drama, break ups (and subsequent passionate make ups), revenge and anguish are all par for the course.

Love Moon Transiting 9th House

Restlessness in a relationship is heightened during this transit and if you are both stuck in a rut, this transit will make the boredom clear. If you're single, this transit can bring a meeting of minds which could develop into a relationship; it can also bring learning experiences of all kinds, including the painful variety.

Love Moon Transiting 10th House

Be careful of your motives in a relationship during this transit. Are you using him? Is he using you? Are you attracted to someone for the right reasons, or the wrong ones? You'll be braver than normal and perhaps taking the initiative in the relationship; you expect to be in charge and there will be sparks if you're not.

Love Moon Transiting 11th House

During this gregarious transit, three can be crowd. However much you'd like to be alone with someone, this transit is a sociable and busy time. Obstacles to your relationship can crop up elsewhere too, in the form of someone's disapproval. However, this is also the most likely transit for a friendship turning into a romance.

Love Moon Transiting 12th House

During this transit, romance can go one of two ways: either you'll be loved up and cocooned in your own little fantasy world together – or you'll be as moody as heck and very difficult to put up with. If you're single, you'll yearn for romance during these few days; if you're in a relationship, you might find that it doesn't quite match up with your expectations. There is a chance of deception too. Try not to lie, or allow yourself to be lied to.

Exercise: Tracking Your Love Moods

Find out which house your moon is transiting today. How does that match up with what you've experienced in love today? Remember to blend in the overall energies of your Moon Sign too. If you can track this every day for one whole moon cycle – 28 days – then at the end of that cycle you'll start to notice patterns repeating. Use the downloadable Moon in Love journal page to keep track, or just make notes in your journal as you go along.

Examples:

Virgo Moon personality when the Love Moon is transiting your 12th House – your desire to be in a relationship could override your normal common sense and discrimination, leading to a risqué encounter or an infatuation with someone from afar.

Cancer Moon personality when the Love Moon is transiting your 5th House – you're feeling much more flirtatious than normal, and you won't be so worried about whether anyone else approves of either your behaviour or your relationship.

Aquarius Moon personality when the Love Moon is transiting your 1st House – it will be much easier for you to tell a boyfriend how you feel during this transit, and your increased emotional openness is a great chance to meet someone new too.

Using the Moon to Help with Love Issues and Decisions

As well as tracking the Moon's movements through your chart and understanding how this can affect your moods and attitude towards love, you can also be more proactive with using the Moon's energies. For most common situations, there are some lunar energies, signs and houses which are more helpful than others, and if you have the chance to plan ahead it helps to know which days might be best for handling certain things. Of course you won't always have a choice, but when you do, try to choose the following moon transits and energies when you:

Start a new relationship – moon in either loving Leo, romantic Libra or your own Moon Sign; moon transiting your 1st or 7th House.

Introduce a new boyfriend to parents – moon in Pisces (for romance) or Capricorn (for maturity), moon transiting your 5th or 7th House.

Tell your family that you're gay – Moon in straightforward Sagittarius or nurturing Cancer, moon transiting your 1st House.

Deepen a relationship – Moon in Taurus (for common sense and permanence) or Scorpio (for passion and intensity); moon transiting your 2nd or 7th House.

Slow down a relationship that's moving too quickly – Moon in detached Aquarius or calm and patient Virgo; moon transiting your 6th or 9th House.

End a relationship – Moon in Aries (for bravery) or Leo (for power and authority); moon transiting your 1st, 6th or 8th House.

End a relationship if hoping to remain friends – Moon in objective Aquarius or rational, sociable Gemini; moon transiting your 5th or 11th House.

Turn a friendship into a relationship – Moon in passionate Scorpio or dreamy Pisces; moon transiting your 7th or 11th House.

Turn down a date – Moon in Cancer (for kindness) or Aquarius (for independence), moon transiting your 1st or 9th House.

Defend your relationship when parents don't approve – Moon in honest Sagittarius or passionate Leo, moon transiting your 4th or

7th House.

Confront a friend who has been flirting with your boyfriend – Moon in Gemini (if you think it was relatively harmless and want to save your friendship) or Scorpio (if you think she meant it), moon transiting your 2nd or 8th House.

Flirt (just for fun) – Moon in either of the two most flirtatious sign, Gemini or Leo, moon transiting your 1st or 5th House.

Flirt (with intent) – Moon in seductive Scorpio or powerful Sagittarius, moon transiting your 7th or 8th House.

Don't panic if the "right" Moon Sign or house transit doesn't fit with what you need or want to do! Any tasks, at any time, will be easier to manage if you refer back to what you already know about your lunar personality and its strengths and weaknesses, both at home and in everyday life. If you have to do something awkward or difficult on a day when the Moon Sign or house transit isn't ideal, find out which sign the Moon will be in on that day, and which of your houses it will be transiting. Think carefully about the energies in play – what can you do to make the most of the Moon's energies, and to minimise any particular problems?

Chapter 9

Your Healthy Moon

The Moon has long been associated with health; through the ages a plethora of beliefs have been built up, some with more evidence than others, about how the Earth's constant companion contributes to our health and well-being. Just as the Moon affects the tides in our oceans, so it is believed to also affect, albeit slightly, the water which makes up the vast majority of each of our bodies. During a Full Moon, it is said that we bleed more easily, and the wisdom of the ages advises against having an operation during the Full Moon, in case the bleeding is not easy to staunch. The Full Moon is also infamous for its alleged links with crazy, wild behaviour – indeed, the word lunacy derives from luna, the Latin for Moon. Many experienced police officers, paramedics and other emergency professionals will tell you that the nights of the Full Moon are always their busiest and most traumatic shifts. Others will argue that the statistics don't bear this out, but still the belief persists.

On a more personal level, the 28-day lunar cycle corresponds closely to the average 28-day menstrual cycle. As you work through this book and become more attuned to the energies and moods of the Moon, you may very well find that your own cycle gradually shifts to align itself with a particular lunar energy, and that your period will always begin when the Moon is in a certain sign. Indeed, learning to live and breathe lunar energies can be a very effective way of regulating erratic periods.

Perhaps most significant, however, is the Moon's psychological affect on our moods and emotions. Your mental health will fluctuate during the course of a year, a month or even a week, with times of joy, times of sadness and times when you simply feel down. Taking a closer look at the lunar energies of health can help you to understand why this is, and to deal better with the inevitable moments of down time. Let's take a look at how the different lunar personalities play a part in our health. You can use the Your Healthy Moon journal sheet, downloadable from the website, or you can create your own journal pages as you work through this chapter.

Your Healthy Aries Moon

Aries energy is extremely fast moving and when your body isn't moving, stress and tension build up. It's essential that you have a healthy – and preferably competitive – outlet for all that energy. Sports of all kinds are a vital tool for maintaining both your physical and mental health. If you're not a team kind of girl, take up a form of solo exercise, even if it's just cycling to and from school every day. Headaches are common for the Aries Moon personality, particularly when you feel frustrated or held back in any way.

Healthy eating: Don't be in such a rush to eat your food. Savour each mouthful and use plenty of strong flavours like garlic, onion, chilli and pepper.

Coping with stress: Focus on your main goal. Strip away any worry which doesn't relate to that one goal and your way ahead will suddenly become much clearer. Cut to the essentials.

Exercise: Yes please! Stay as physically active as possible. All kinds of sports are good for you, but warrior type activities like martial arts hold a particular appeal.

Beauty: Wear red and other dramatic colours. Choose easy hairstyles and time saving beauty products so that you don't have to spend hours each day in a quest to look good – you simply don't have the patience for that!

Most energy when the Moon is in: Aries, Leo, Sagittarius

Least energy when the Moon is in: Libra

Working with Your Healthy Aries Moon: Try these journal

prompts on your Healthy Moon sheet.

- For a month, plot your general well-being levels each day. Give each day a rating of 1–10, with 10 for when you feel on top of the world and 1 for when you feel low or depressed. Of course, events in life will influence your mood, but try to give a rating for your own inner mood, regardless of what's going on around you. At the end of the month, see if you can spot any patterns. Were you "up" during the Moon's transits through your fellow fire signs, and "down" when the Moon was in your opposite sign of Libra?
- How important is looking good to you? Write a paragraph about how much time/energy/money you spend on your beauty, and why. Can you see how that matches your Moon Sign energies?
- How do you normally cope with stress? Think of a stressful situation and write down what you did to try to make yourself feel better. Is there a way in which the stress strategy for your sign could help you cope better next time?

Your Healthy Taurus Moon

Taurus energy is quite placid and laid back, and indeed you do manage to avoid a great deal of stress with your easy come, easy go approach to life. A tendency towards physical laziness and a liking for food can have negative impacts on your health, however. You have a lot of common sense and will find it easy to stick to exercise routines or a healthy diet once you get started, but that initial motivation isn't always easy to find – and the more someone else pushes you to take better care of yourself, the more your stubborn streak will refuse.

Healthy eating: Not so much of the chocolate and comfort food! Berry fruits will give you plenty of sweetness and have a sense of indulgence too, so use those as your treats instead.

Coping with stress: Change is much less alarming if you plan. Instead of fighting it, put your energy into making a detailed plan of what you will do when the change comes.

Exercise: Not if you can help it! Strength sports and weight training appeal to you though, as does anything graceful like dance, yoga or gymnastics.

Beauty: Wear pale blue and pale green. Choose the best quality beauty products you can afford, even if that means having fewer products overall. Think quality, not quantity – and that includes how much make-up you wear.

Most energy when the Moon is in: Taurus, Virgo, Capricorn

Least energy when the Moon is in: Scorpio

Working with Your Healthy Taurus Moon: Try these journal prompts on your Healthy Moon sheet.

- For a month, plot your general well-being levels each day. Give each day a rating of 1–10, with 10 for when you feel on top of the world and 1 for when you feel low or depressed. Of course, events in life will influence your mood, but try to give a rating for your own inner mood, regardless of what's going on around you. At the end of the month, see if you can spot any patterns. Were you "up" during the Moon's transits through your fellow earth signs, and "down" when the Moon was in your opposite sign of Scorpio?
- How important is looking good to you? Write a paragraph about how much time/energy/money you spend on your beauty, and why. Can you see how that matches your Moon Sign energies?
- How do you normally cope with stress? Think of a stressful situation and write down what you did to try to make yourself feel better. Is there a way in which the stress strategy for your sign could help you cope better next time?

Your Healthy Gemini Moon

You don't tend to suffer many problems with your physical health, apart from a tendency to colds, but your stress levels can easily go through the roof, especially since you bottle up your feelings and don't talk them through. Eating sensibly comes naturally to you, and you enjoy most individual sports, but boredom is a problem when you're trying to set up or maintain new healthy habits. Variety is essential for your psychological well-being, so keep on the go with a mixture of sports, hobbies and pastimes, rather than devoting yourself to one.

Healthy eating: You make sensible choices instinctively – well done you! Top up your essential vitamins with plenty of nuts, seeds and legumes.

Coping with stress: Talk! Hiding your feelings really does not help. If you can't talk about what you're feeling, write it down or send a note; the important thing is to get your feelings into the open air.

Exercise: Spice it up. You'd enjoy the variety of athletics, or create your own mix and match exercise regimes with a group of friends – socialising while working out will make it easy for you to stick to your positive habits.

Beauty: Wear yellow if you can stand it, or metallic hues. Learn several different hair styling techniques so you don't get bored with your look, and experiment with make-up free looks too.

Most energy when the Moon is in: Gemini, Libra, Aquarius

Least energy when the Moon is in: Sagittarius

Working with Your Healthy Gemini Moon: Try these journal prompts on your Healthy Moon sheet.

- For a month, plot your general well-being levels each day. Give each day a rating of 1–10, with 10 for when you feel on top of the world and 1 for when you feel low or depressed. Of course, events in life will influence your mood, but try to give a rating for your own inner mood, regardless of what's going on around you. At the end of the month, see if you can spot any patterns. Were you "up" during the Moon's transits through your fellow air signs, and "down" when the Moon was in your opposite sign of Sagittarius?

- How important is looking good to you? Write a paragraph about how much time/energy/money you spend on your beauty, and why. Can you see how that matches your Moon Sign energies?
- How do you normally cope with stress? Think of a stressful situation and write down what you did to try to make yourself feel better. Is there a way in which the stress strategy for your sign could help you cope better next time?

Your Healthy Cancer Moon

Worry and anxiety are your biggest potential health problems. Your bodily systems are very susceptible to your mental health and keeping both body and mind well together is quite some task. You might have digestion troubles, and your menstrual cycle is also heavily affected by any stress you feel. It's usually easy for others to tell how you're feeling by how you look – when you're up, you take a great deal of trouble over your appearance, but when you're depressed you simply cannot be bothered.

Healthy eating: Avoid spicy foods with that delicate digestion. You enjoy fish and milk, both of which play a crucial role in keeping your system balanced. Drink plenty of water and avoid tea, coffee and fizzy drinks.

Coping with stress: Your imagination can be your worst enemy – turn it into your best friend instead by using creative visualisation techniques to focus on the best that can happen instead of the worst.

Exercise: You don't mind exercise, but your changing moods make it difficult for you to stick to it. Joining a swimming club or watersports team will help with motivation.

Beauty: Wear silver, grey and blue. Loose, floaty fabrics reflect your imagination and your nurturing nature. Choose cruelty-free beauty products so that you can look good with a clear conscience.

Most energy when the Moon is in: Cancer, Scorpio, Pisces

Least energy when the Moon is in: Capricorn

Working with Your Healthy Cancer Moon: Try these journal prompts on your Healthy Moon sheet.

- For a month, plot your general well-being levels each day. Give each day a rating of 1–10, with 10 for when you feel on top of the world and 1 for when you feel low or depressed. Of course, events in life will influence your mood, but try to give a rating for your own inner mood, regardless of what's going on around you. At the end of the month, see if you can spot any patterns. Were you "up" during the Moon's transits through your fellow water signs, and "down" when the Moon was in your opposite sign of Capricorn?
- How important is looking good to you? Write a paragraph about how much time/energy/money you spend on your beauty, and why. Can you see how that matches your Moon Sign energies?
- How do you normally cope with stress? Think of a stressful situation and write down what you did to try to make yourself feel better. Is there a way in which the stress strategy for your sign could help you cope better next time?

Your Healthy Leo Moon

With a strong constitution and plenty of vibrant energy, your overall health is great. You do try to pack an awful lot into your life, though, and as a result you are frequently very tired. Plenty of good quality sleep is essential, otherwise it will start to show in back strain and muscle aches. Competitive and team sports appeal to that dynamic Leo energy and you also enjoy dramatic and unusual activities like extreme sports. Psychologically, you're robust and generally even tempered, but if you feel that your control or authority is threatened, you can become insular and moody.

Healthy eating: A tendency to skip breakfast isn't helping your tiredness. Cereal or toast in the morning is a must so that your blood sugar levels stay stable until lunch time.

Coping with stress: Try not to assume that you always know best. Make sure you're your voice is heard during times of stress, but offer your opinion without trying to enforce it. Accepting someone else's lead for a change soothes your stress.

Exercise: You're keen, provided you can win! Your flair for drama enjoys archery, and fencing – something where the tools of the trade make a statement in themselves!

Beauty: Wear warm sunshine colours. Since you insist on looking immaculate, factor in plenty of time for your beauty regime; you can't bear to cut corners there. Sunshine heals your skin, but avoid sunbeds and always wear sunscreen.

Most energy when the Moon is in: Aries, Leo, Sagittarius

Least energy when the Moon is in: Aquarius

Working with Your Healthy Leo Moon: Try these journal prompts on your Healthy Moon sheet.

- For a month, plot your general well-being levels each day. Give each day a rating of 1–10, with 10 for when you feel on top of the world and 1 for when you feel low or depressed. Of course, events in life will influence your mood, but try to give a rating for your own inner mood, regardless of what's going on around you. At the end of the month, see if you can spot any patterns. Were you "up" during the Moon's transits through your fellow fire signs, and "down" when the Moon was in your opposite sign of Aquarius?

- How important is looking good to you? Write a paragraph about how much time/energy/money you spend on your beauty, and why. Can you see how that matches your Moon Sign energies?
- How do you normally cope with stress? Think of a stressful situation and write down what you did to try to make yourself feel better. Is there a way in which the stress strategy for your sign could help you cope better next time?

Your Healthy Virgo Moon

Being highly critical of yourself, you can be your own worst enemy when it comes to health. You're very interested in health, healing and alternative therapies, but your own stress levels can reach high enough levels to cause digestion upsets, constipation, migraines and severe depression. It's essential that you learn to love yourself and try to silence your inner critic for a while. When it comes to sports, you are a little too reserved to enjoy team sports, but you do enjoy running, cycling and tennis. Learning to meditate will help enormously in calming your nerves.

Healthy eating: You excel at making healthy eating choices and you enjoy a vegetarian, vegan or wholefood diet, being highly aware of the significance of what you put into your body.

Coping with stress: Take a dual pronged approach to calming your mind and body. Use your analytical, rational talents to realise that the worst is unlikely to happen; use meditation or breathing exercises to physically soothe your body.

Exercise: You enjoy exercise you can do alone and in your own time, when it suits your lifestyle, rather than in a club or group. Walking, hiking, running or even a home exercise bike are all good choices.

Beauty: Wear forest green and chocolate brown. You like the natural look, avoiding too much make-up, but choose pure, allergy free skin care basics to build a daily beauty routine.

Most energy when the Moon is in: Taurus, Virgo, Capricorn

Least energy when the Moon is in: Pisces

Working with Your Healthy Virgo Moon: Try these journal prompts on your Healthy Moon sheet.

- For a month, plot your general well-being levels each day. Give each day a rating of 1–10, with 10 for when you feel on top of the world and 1 for when you feel low or depressed. Of course, events in life will influence your mood, but try to give a rating for your own inner mood, regardless of what's going on around you. At the end of the month, see if you can spot any patterns. Were you "up" during the Moon's transits through your fellow earth signs, and "down" when the Moon was in your opposite sign of Pisces?
- How important is looking good to you? Write a paragraph about how much time/energy/money you spend on your beauty, and why. Can you see how that matches your Moon Sign energies?
- How do you normally cope with stress? Think of a stressful situation and write down what you did to try to make yourself feel better. Is there a way in which the stress strategy for your sign could help you cope better next time?

Your Healthy Libra Moon

Your biggest health challenge is a lack of self-discipline, whether it's over your eating choices or your aversion to exercise. Psychologically, you are also heavily influenced by the moods of other people, so living in a stressful environment can have long-term implications for your health. It's vital that you avoid negative people and situations whenever possible, since you soak them up like a sponge. You typically have a slow metabolism, so take care to eat little but often in order to kick-start it and to keep your blood sugar levels from fluctuating wildly.

Healthy eating: Don't deny yourself your treats, but do take more of an interest in the eating choices you're making. Instead of automatically reaching for what you always have, explore healthier treats like grapes or apple slices.

Coping with stress: The absence of a decision is still a decision, you know. You can't sit on the fence forever. Making a choice – whichever choice – and sticking to it will always eliminate part of the stress, so do not procrastinate for too long.

Exercise: Why? You struggle to see the point of exercise, so the key is finding something you love to do which happens to be physical. Ice skating is typical of what would appeal to your sense of beauty.

Beauty: Wear pretty shades of pink and pastels. Getting your hair or nails done professionally is essential to your self-esteem, so don't feel guilty about it. Meanwhile, learn some of the techniques to do at home, so you don't always have to spend so much.

Most energy when the Moon is in: Gemini, Libra, Aquarius

Least energy when the Moon is in: Aries

Working with Your Healthy Libra Moon: Try these journal prompts on your Healthy Moon sheet.

- For a month, plot your general well-being levels each day. Give each day a rating of 1–10, with 10 for when you feel on top of the world and 1 for when you feel low or depressed. Of course, events in life will influence your mood, but try to give a rating for your own inner mood, regardless of what's going on around you. At the end of the month, see if you can spot any patterns. Were you "up" during the Moon's transits through your fellow air signs, and "down" when the Moon was in your opposite sign of Aries?

- How important is looking good to you? Write a paragraph about how much time/energy/money you spend on your beauty, and why. Can you see how that matches your Moon Sign energies?
- How do you normally cope with stress? Think of a stressful situation and write down what you did to try to make yourself feel better. Is there a way in which the stress strategy for your sign could help you cope better next time?

Your Healthy Scorpio Moon

Intense Scorpio Moon emotions need careful handling if they're not to have an adverse effect on your health. Talking through your feelings is essential and it's also helpful for you to have a hobby you're passionate about, as a way of redirecting emotional energy. You go through phases when it comes to exercise, either not wanting to bother at all or becoming obsessive about it; similarly with your diet, you'll either eat whatever you want, whenever you want, or try to deny yourself everything at once. Moderation is the key.

Healthy eating: Avoid fad diets, crash diets and indeed any other kind of restrictive diet. Use your common sense to cut back on unhealthy items, but don't get so hung on up on what you're eating that it becomes a chore.

Coping with stress: Action is important, rather than sitting around brooding. Decide what you want to see happen, and then deliberately take one or two steps towards making it happen. Getting in control in this way will eliminate some of your anxieties.

Exercise: You're drawn to meaningful forms of exercise, especially those with a spiritual background like martial arts, yoga or exotic dance. Keep an exercise diary so that you can spot when you're overdoing it.

Beauty: Wear dark reds and purple. You love smoky, smouldering make-up but let your skin breathe with a few days off. Sophisticated hairstyles suit you, as does very long hair.

Most energy when the Moon is in: Cancer, Scorpio, Pisces

Least energy when the Moon is in: Taurus

Working with Your Healthy Scorpio Moon: Try these journal prompts on your Healthy Moon sheet.

- For a month, plot your general well-being levels each day. Give each day a rating of 1–10, with 10 for when you feel on top of the world and 1 for when you feel low or depressed. Of course, events in life will influence your mood, but try to give a rating for your own inner mood, regardless of what's going on around you. At the end of the month, see if you can spot any patterns. Were you "up" during the Moon's transits through your fellow water signs, and "down" when the Moon was in your opposite sign of Taurus?
- How important is looking good to you? Write a paragraph about how much time/energy/money you spend on your beauty, and why. Can you see how that matches your Moon Sign energies?
- How do you normally cope with stress? Think of a stressful situation and write down what you did to try to make yourself feel better. Is there a way in which the stress strategy for your sign could help you cope better next time?

Your Healthy Sagittarius Moon

Energetic, open and sporty, you don't usually have a problem with laziness, and keeping fit and active is a natural part of your being. You are somewhat reckless by nature, though, and injuries from sports or just from pure carelessness are common. Psychologically, you don't worry a great deal about anything and take life as it comes. This is a healthy attitude, but when your freedom is blocked or you're expected to conform to rules which don't suit you, you can become inwardly aggressive, almost turning on yourself, even to the point of self-harm or deliberate risk-taking.

Healthy eating: Try to cut down a little on red meat, replacing it with white meat and fish. Learn that it's OK to eat the foods you love; you don't have to be too strict with yourself over your healthy diet.

Coping with stress: Treat stress like the boggarts from Harry Potter – use humour as your weapon. You are blessed with being able to find a funny side to absolutely everything, which will relax you and make the object of your stress much less challenging.

Exercise: You're always on the go, but your favourite sports will be outdoor ones, particularly horse riding or cross-country running – choose exercise which gives you a sense of freedom.

Beauty: Wear dark blue, navy and burgundy. Don't be taken in by expensive creams and products which promise the earth – you're a little gullible when it comes to beauty when all you really need are a good selection of the basics.

Most energy when the Moon is in: Aries, Leo, Sagittarius

Least energy when the Moon is in: Gemini

Working with Your Healthy Sagittarius Moon: Try these journal prompts on your Healthy Moon sheet.

- For a month, plot your general well-being levels each day. Give each day a rating of 1–10, with 10 for when you feel on top of the world and 1 for when you feel low or depressed. Of course, events in life will influence your mood, but try to give a rating for your own inner mood, regardless of what's going on around you. At the end of the month, see if you can spot any patterns. Were you "up" during the Moon's transits through your fellow fire signs, and "down" when the Moon was in your opposite sign of Gemini?

- How important is looking good to you? Write a paragraph about how much time/energy/money you spend on your beauty, and why. Can you see how that matches your Moon Sign energies?
- How do you normally cope with stress? Think of a stressful situation and write down what you did to try to make yourself feel better. Is there a way in which the stress strategy for your sign could help you cope better next time?

Your Healthy Capricorn Moon

Keeping your emotions under control and well hidden takes a lot of energy, and it's in muscle and joint pain that your emotional upheavals are felt the most, as well as in skin break outs. Exercise which promotes flexibility is vital. You don't particularly enjoy keeping fit and healthy, but you are supremely sensible about it and will stick carefully to a routine. Make sure that what you're sticking to so valiantly is actually good for you, however – you are a bit over-keen to follow the latest celeb diet; if they're doing it, it must be right, no? No.

Healthy eating: You do need more calcium than some other Moon Signs, so eat plenty of dairy products. A love of starchy potatoes and pasta needn't be a problem for maintaining a healthy weight provided you don't overdo it.

Coping with stress: Your natural pessimism is the biggest problem when you're under stress. You always assume the worst. Make a conscious decision to find something – anything – positive about the situation, and focus instead on that.

Exercise: Choose an exercise or sport which uses all of your joints but which is low impact. Climbing, swimming, yoga or tai chi are possibilities, although you also work very well as part of a team in any sport.

Beauty: Wear dark green, grey, brown and earth colours. You tend to regard make-up and luxury products as a waste of both time and money, but it will cheer you up enormously to be looking your best, so allow yourself an indulgence now and then.
Most energy when the Moon is in: Taurus, Virgo, Capricorn

Least energy when the Moon is in: Cancer

Working with Your Healthy Capricorn Moon: Try these journal prompts on your Healthy Moon sheet.

- For a month, plot your general well-being levels each day. Give each day a rating of 1–10, with 10 for when you feel on top of the world and 1 for when you feel low or depressed. Of course, events in life will influence your mood, but try to give a rating for your own inner mood, regardless of what's going on around you. At the end of the month, see if you can spot any patterns. Were you "up" during the Moon's transits through your fellow earth signs, and "down" when the Moon was in your opposite sign of Cancer?
- How important is looking good to you? Write a paragraph about how much time/energy/money you spend on your beauty, and why. Can you see how that matches your Moon Sign energies?
- How do you normally cope with stress? Think of a stressful situation and write down what you did to try to make yourself feel better. Is there a way in which the stress strategy for your sign could help you cope better next time?

Your Healthy Aquarius Moon

Your energy levels are erratic, and your behaviour towards your health follows suit – one day you'll pour all of your energy into looking and feeling good, while the next day you couldn't care less. You are also quite an awkward patient, and won't help yourself with medicines etc, preferring to suffer on. Very conscious of alternative health and cutting-edge medical theories, you're somewhat distrustful of standard doctors and will usually ignore the advice you're given. Try to adopt a more consistent approach to exercise, instead of exhausting yourself and then doing nothing for a week!

Healthy eating: Fruit is the key to maintaining optimum health in your diet. Apples, pears and other tree fruits are ideal, as are citrus fruits; the more the merrier. Avoid overly processed food – or go vegan!

Coping with stress: You find it hard when change hangs over your head for ages, and much easier when it happens quickly or out of the blue. Try to avoid asking questions you don't really want the answers to, as this will only prolong the time you have to worry.

Exercise: Although you'd prefer to go paragliding or scuba diving, you need to choose something more accessible that you can do regularly. How about skating, gymnastics or hockey?

Beauty: Wear electric, shocking splashes of colour. Change your make-up style often and invent your own look rather than following trends or – worse – instructions. Do your own thing.

Most energy when the Moon is in: Gemini, Libra, Aquarius

Least energy when the Moon is in: Leo

Working with Your Healthy Aquarius Moon: Try these journal prompts on your Healthy Moon sheet.

- For a month, plot your general well-being levels each day. Give each day a rating of 1–10, with 10 for when you feel on top of the world and 1 for when you feel low or depressed. Of course, events in life will influence your mood, but try to give a rating for your own inner mood, regardless of what's going on around you. At the end of the month, see if you can spot any patterns. Were you "up" during the Moon's transits through your fellow air signs, and "down" when the Moon was in your opposite sign of Leo?

- How important is looking good to you? Write a paragraph about how much time/energy/money you spend on your beauty, and why. Can you see how that matches your Moon Sign energies?
- How do you normally cope with stress? Think of a stressful situation and write down what you did to try to make yourself feel better. Is there a way in which the stress strategy for your sign could help you cope better next time?

Your Healthy Pisces Moon

You are an exceptionally sensitive soul and easily prone to bouts of depression, even over world events which do not directly affect you. Fortunately, however, you find it easy to express your emotions and you are usually able to talk things over and drag yourself back up again. Where you do need to be careful, however, is with an attraction to alcohol and drugs as a form of escapism. You're easily led, and easily addicted – do be careful. Exercise is not something you particularly enjoy, but you do like to swim, so focus on that.

Healthy eating: Generally, you eat well, but when you're feeling low you rely on sweet things to lift your mood. Try to choose healthy foods which will release the sugar you need, but slowly: porridge, for instance, or fruit.

Coping with stress: You can quickly become overwhelmed with stress to the point that you can see no way out. Yet there is always a solution. Get plenty of sleep and you will find that your dreams offer some answers – and write down your fears, since they always seem more manageable on paper than in your head.

Exercise: Swimming, swimming and more swimming – with

some other water-based activities just for a change. Would you like to learn to row or to sail? Both will get you into the fresh air and blow away some blues.

Beauty: Wear turquoise, cream and sea blue. Go for soft, barely there make-up as too heavy a look drowns out your delicate beauty. Perfume is important to you, but spend a while choosing a scent that doesn't give you a headache after ten minutes!

Most energy when the Moon is in: Cancer, Scorpio, Pisces

Least energy when the Moon is in: Virgo

Working with Your Healthy Pisces Moon: Try these journal prompts on your Healthy Moon sheet.

- For a month, plot your general well-being levels each day. Give each day a rating of 1–10, with 10 for when you feel on top of the world and 1 for when you feel low or depressed. Of course, events in life will influence your mood, but try to give a rating for your own inner mood, regardless of what's going on around you. At the end of the month, see if you can spot any patterns. Were you "up" during the Moon's transits through your fellow water signs, and "down" when the Moon was in your opposite sign of Virgo?
- How important is looking good to you? Write a paragraph about how much time/energy/money you spend on your beauty, and why. Can you see how that matches your Moon Sign energies?
- How do you normally cope with stress? Think of a stressful situation and write down what you did to try to make yourself feel better. Is there a way in which the stress strategy for your sign could help you cope better next time?

Your 12 Health and Beauty Moods

As the Moon progresses through the 12 houses each month, your mood and energy levels will subtly change. You will always remain true to your Moon Sign, but within the background flavour that your Moon Sign provides, your focus will shift.

Health and Beauty Moon Transiting 1st House

You're very aware of your health during this transit, and acutely aware of your own appearance. It's a fabulous time for a makeover, a new look, a haircut or a change of make-up style, and also a very good time to make positive changes to your lifestyle which will result in better health. Willpower is strong now.

Health and Beauty Moon Transiting 2nd House

Sticking with the tried and tested, you're comfy with your own look during these few days, but if anyone comments adversely on your appearance you will take it very much to heart. If you have difficulties speaking up for yourself during this transit, or if you feel that you're not in control of a situation, this can manifest itself physically as a sore throat or lump in your throat. You're not as energetic as normal.

Health and Beauty Moon Transiting 3rd House

You'll value looks far more than anything deeper during this transit, and a superficial need to look good can override almost everything else. It's a good transit for handling stress, however, since you'll find it easier than normal to talk through problems, share difficult emotions and generally clear emotional blockages and hang-ups.

Health and Beauty Moon Transiting 4th House

During this transit, worries can take on a life of their own. If you already find it difficult to express your emotions, this transit can make that even harder, leading to repressed feelings and associated health problems, like mystery stomach aches and headaches. Plenty of fresh air is essential during these few days, as is a sympathetic friend or family member who can "read" how you feel without having to be told.

Health and Beauty Moon Transiting 5th House

A very healthy and robust few days, both for your physical health and your mental health. Laughter is the great healer at this time and a good giggle can sweep away worries as if they never existed. It's also a fun time to experiment with your look and to be more daring with your appearance. Just don't go doing anything you can't reverse, because you won't necessarily like it once this transit has passed!

Health and Beauty Moon Transiting 6th House

This is the most significant health transit of all, and a hugely positive time for dealing with all kinds of physical health concerns. It's a particularly strong time for resolving to eat better or for dramatic changes like going vegetarian. It's also the perfect time for kicking bad habits. It's a slightly trickier story for mental health, however, with this being a time when disrupted routines can lead to huge stress, and when an overactive imagination can make people ill. Dredge up whatever common sense you have to earth and anchor your worries before they run away with you.

Health and Beauty Moon Transiting 7th House

You'll care a lot about how you look during this transit, but only because you want to please someone else. Likewise, you'll do your best to eat better or to kick a bad habit – for someone else. That's very noble, but unfortunately unlikely to stick unless and until you're doing it for yourself. Disruptions to your emotional security now can lead to skin break outs, coughs and colds. Make sure you balance your waking activities with plenty of sleep.

Health and Beauty Moon Transiting 8th House

If you're going through an emotional upheaval, this transit will intensify it. Even relatively stress-free periods of life can take a darker turn during these few days. The good news is that it's also a powerful time for taking control of your own feelings and your health. Make sweeping, dramatic changes if you want to. Adopt a "why not?" strategy. Be daring, because hiding away will only make you feel worse.

Health and Beauty Moon Transiting 9th House

Boredom with sports, exercise routines, diets and, well, just about everything else means that this is a tricky transit for staying well. Allow yourself a few days off so that you can start again refreshed and with new enthusiasm. Forcing yourself to stick to something you don't like during this transit will have knock-on effects on your mood for days. It's a positive time for going without make-up and letting your skin breathe, and for giving your hair a rest too. Aim for the natural, outdoor girl look.

Health and Beauty Moon Transiting 10th House

You'll be cross with yourself over health issues during this transit, berating yourself for not exercising enough, not eating well enough and generally falling short of your own high expectations – especially if you did have some "time off" during the 9th House Moon. Chill out. It's hard to relax and switch off during this transit but meditation and relaxation techniques can help.

Health and Beauty Moon Transiting 11th House

So long as exercise can be a sociable thing, you'll happily run, walk, cycle, jog, play, swim and bounce your way to fitness during these few days – in company, of course. Your mood is generally gregarious and optimistic, so it's a healthy emotional time too. Your feelings are on an even keel and it's much easier now to climb out of depression and to find optimism again.

Health and Beauty Moon Transiting 12th House
Overwhelming emotions can spell depression, anxiety and severe mood swings during this transit. Don't fight this. It's OK – healthy, even – to cry, and it's perfectly fine to feel down for a short while. Don't beat yourself up about it. Do whatever you need to do to make yourself feel comforted and loved, and don't try to take on too many challenges. When all is going well, this is a wonderful transit for beauty, with your skin, hair and eyes taking on an almost mystical shimmer.

Exercise: Tracking Your Health

Find out which house your moon is transiting today. How does that match up with what you've experienced with your health and well-being today? Remember to blend in the overall energies of your Moon Sign too. If you can track this every day for one whole moon cycle – 28 days – then at the end of that cycle you'll start to notice patterns repeating. Use the downloadable Healthy Moon journal page to keep track, or just make notes in your journal as you go along.

Examples:

Virgo Moon personality when the Health and Beauty Moon is transiting the 12th House – you'll feel extremely anxious about situations beyond your control, but if you can avoid feeling silly for feeling that way, you can start to gradually recognise that you have a right to feel anxious… and that there are practical solutions you can try.

Gemini Moon personality when the Health and Beauty Moon is transiting the 1st House – a wonderfully upbeat few days, perfect for holding a makeover party or for dissecting the latest celeb hairstyles in depth.

Leo Moon personality when the Health and Beauty Moon is transiting the 10th House – you'll be annoyed with yourself for looking less than immaculate – but if you ask a friend, they'll probably tell you that they prefer your more natural look and that you're worrying over nothing.

Using the Moon to Help with Your Physical and Mental Well-being

As well as tracking the Moon's movements through your chart and understanding how this can affect your health, you can also be more proactive with using the Moon's energies. For most common situations, there are some lunar energies, signs and houses which are more helpful than others, and if you have the chance to plan ahead it helps to know which days might be best for handling certain things. Of course you won't always have a choice, but when you do, try to choose the following moon transits and energies when you:

Go vegetarian or vegan – Moon in either humanitarian Aquarius or idealistic Sagittarius, Moon transiting your 3rd House (if parents won't mind) or 1st House (if they will).

Do something very energetic – Moon in your own Moon Sign or a sign of the same element (water, earth, air or fire), Moon transiting your 1st or 5th House.

Catch up on overdue sleep – Moon in sleepy Pisces or indulgent Libra, Moon transiting your 12th or 7th House.

Have a makeover – Moon in your own sign, or in Aries (for courage), Leo (for style) or Scorpio (for drama), Moon transiting your 1st House.

Kick a bad habit – Moon in Capricorn (for willpower), Virgo (for common sense) or Taurus (for constancy), Moon transiting your 1st, 6th or 8th House.

Visit the doctor – Moon in open and honest Sagittarius, or advice-heeding Cancer, Moon transiting your 2nd or 6th House.

Visit the dentist – Moon in Capricorn (which rules teeth) or Aries (for bravery), Moon transiting your 3rd or 11th House.

Try an alternative therapy – Moon in open-minded Aquarius or health conscious Virgo, Moon transiting your 5th or 6th House.

Talk through a difficult emotional problem – Moon in Gemini (for ease of communication) or Scorpio (for emotional depth), Moon transiting your 3rd House.

Don't panic if the "right" Moon Sign or house transit doesn't fit with what you need or want to do! Any tasks, at any time, will be easier to manage if you refer back to what you already know about your lunar personality and its strengths and weaknesses, both at home and in everyday life. If you have to do something awkward or difficult on a day when the Moon Sign or house transit isn't ideal, find out which sign the Moon will be in on that day, and which of your houses it will be transiting. Think carefully about the energies in play – what can you do to make the most of the Moon's energies, and to minimise any particular problems?

Chapter 10

More Moon Surfing

Congratulations! If you've got this far, you've learnt a great deal about lunar astrology: you now know what sign and house your natal Moon is in and what that means for you. You're able to track the Moon's progress through your astrological houses on a daily basis, and to understand and work out its effect on your mood and emotions in different situations and at different times. You also understand the significance of New Moons, Full Moons and eclipses, and you can take a good stab at working out the best lunar signs and houses for you to work on all sorts of activities and problems.

But what else can you do, if you're comfortable with all the techniques used in this book? Let's have brief look at some further things you can try.

1. Aspects from the Transiting Moon to Your Natal Planets

So far, we've mostly concentrated on the monthly journey of the Moon through your astrological houses. As it makes that journey, completing a full circuit of the zodiac every 28 days, it forms particular angles to every other planet in your natal chart at different times. We call these angles aspects. There are many significant types of aspect, but as a brief taster here we'll just look at two: the conjunction and the opposition, and we'll only consider these aspects from the transiting Moon to your natal Sun and your natal Moon.

A conjunction is when two planets occupy the same place or nearly the same place, as seen from Earth. An opposition is when the two planets, as seen from Earth, are literally opposite one another, 180° apart. Now of course, there is only one Moon and one Sun, but when we say your "natal" Moon or Sun we mean the position those planets (and yes, I know, neither the Sun nor the Moon is a planet, but astrologers call them planets for convenience!) occupied at your time of birth. So we're looking for moments when the transiting Moon makes a conjunction or opposition to the place in your natal chart where the Sun and the Moon were at your birth.

Look back at the chart you filled in when you first found your natal Moon and its house position. The same data that you looked up to find out your Moon Sign will also have given you your Sun sign (which you probably already knew) and the degree position of your Sun, eg 12° Libra. Got it? Good. Add the Sun to your chart. Now it should be easy for you to see when the transiting Moon will be conjunct your natal Sun or your natal Moon – when it returns to the same sign. The transiting Moon will be in opposition to your natal Moon and your natal Sun when it's in the opposite sign to each of them.

Example:

Jo's natal Sun is at 12° Libra and her natal Moon is at 2° Sagittarius.

The transiting Moon will be conjunct her natal Sun when it is in Libra, and conjunct her natal Moon when it's in Sagittarius. The transiting Moon will be in opposition to her natal Sun when it's in Aries, and in opposition to her natal Sun when it's in Gemini.

What does it mean? Well:

Transiting Moon conjunct Natal Moon – this day or two marks your monthly lunar birthday. You will be at your most emotional and sensitive of the whole month, both for better and for worse. You'll be quick to laugh and quick to cry; very easily hurt but blessed with an incredible imagination and intuition and a high level of psychic ability.

Transiting Moon opposition Natal Moon – these couple of days are highly emotionally volatile and often very challenging. Your instinctive needs and wants, as symbolised by your natal Moon, are in direct conflict with the energies of the current transiting Moon. You'll often find your way blocked for a couple of days, and it can be an extremely frustrating time. Expect all kinds of feelings to bubble up from out of the blue, and for emotions you didn't even know you had to demand your attention.

Transiting Moon conjunct Natal Sun – this is your own personal New Moon moment. Regardless what phase the actual Moon is currently in, whether new or full, waxing or waning – for your psyche, it's a New Moon. As the transiting Moon's energies blend with all of the potential of your natural Sun sign, it's a hugely powerful time for you and absolutely perfect for new starts, seizing the initiative and asking for what you want and need. You'll be more confident than normal and very emotionally balanced, which should lead to a great feeling of inner calm and well-being.

Transiting Moon opposition Natal Sun – and this is your own personal Full Moon day, and a highly challenging day it can be too. Your ego, symbolised by your natal Sun sign, is now in directly conflict with the emotional energies of the transiting Moon, potentially leading to confusion, turmoil and ill thought through actions. This is a day to stay under the covers if you can, or at the very least to be aware that you are likely to feel angry, frustrated and ill at ease, just for a short while.

See if you can track these four days via your chart for a couple of months. Make notes on how you feel on each of the days, and blend your knowledge so far with your knowledge of which house the transiting Moon is affecting on those days. How can you make the most of these four major dates, or minimise the tensions they regularly bring?

2. Comparing Your Chart with Someone Else's

In astrology, the art of comparing one person's natal chart with someone else's, in order to gain insight into their relationship, is called synastry. It's a fascinating branch of astrology, but much too complex to cover here. However, there is one little trick which is easy to do with the tools and knowledge you have, and which can give you a quick flash of insight into your current relationships (provided you have the other person's birth data!).

Look up the birth data of your friend, parent, boyfriend or whoever, exactly as you looked up your own at the beginning of this book. Now, put their natal Moon into your own chart wheel, as if it were your own. Use a different colour so you can clearly tell which Moon is yours and which is theirs. Yes? Good. Now, you're going to temporarily re-number the houses. Pretend that the house your own Moon is in is the first house. Write a nice big number 1 in there. Now, count anticlockwise from there around the rest of the houses, numbering them up to 12. Which "new" house is your friend's Moon in?

Look back to the lunar house interpretations in Chapter 2. With a bit of creative imagination and astrological flair, can you apply that interpretation to your relationship with your friend/parent/boyfriend? For instance, if his Moon is in the "new" 2nd House, that would indicate that you are possessive of him; if her Moon is in the "new" 4th House, that might suggest that you are very close but that you struggle to be independent of one another; her Moon in the "new" 9th House would indicate a positive, healthy friendship that stretches you both – and so on.

This technique is called derived houses; although it's a very quick and simple thing to do, it can throw an interesting light on relationships of all kinds!

3. Spotting Patterns

Once you've been keeping your lunar journal for a while, take some time out to look back on your findings and see if you can spot any patterns. Did your mood always fall when the Moon was in a particular sign? Did you find yourself rowing with others more often during the Moon's transit through a particular house? What about your happiest days? What do they have in common, astrologically-wise? Did you always feel at your best a day or two after a New Moon, or when the Moon was conjunct your natal Moon?

Throughout this book, we've focused almost exclusively on the Moon, with occasional mention of the Sun – but of course, Mercury, Venus, Mars, Jupiter, Saturn, Uranus, Neptune and Pluto are all also present in your natal chart somewhere, and playing a significant part in your astrological make-up. Without calculating and interpreting a whole chart, an astrologer can only ever give you part of the picture. However, when you do spot patterns like those I've mentioned, it's almost always an indicator that the Moon's transit is activating/affecting something significant in the rest of your chart. If you choose to learn more about astrology (and I hope you will!) then bear this in mind as you learn about the rest of your chart – the patterns you've spotted via your lunar journal will be an excellent starting point for understanding your whole chart.

Which brings me to:

4. Learn More About Astrology!

If you've been bitten by the astrology bug, the good news is that there are dozens of websites which can help you learn more, free of charge, and dozens more books which can guide you through learning astrology as a fascinating hobby or even an eventual career choice.

To start with, use the site you found your Moon Sign data from to find out which sign all your other planets are in. You can then plot those on to your chart wheel and you'll discover which house they're in. Many websites will give you quick'n'easy interpretations if you just google something like "Saturn in 3rd

House" or "Venus in 12th House". Take off on a journey of discovery, and see what you can find out about yourself – and the rest of mankind! Bon voyage!

Dodona Books offers a broad spectrum of divination systems to suit all, including Astrology, Tarot, Runes, Ogham, Palmistry, Dream Interpretation, Scrying, Dowsing, I Ching, Numerology, Angels and Faeries, Tasseomancy and Introspection.